A Brief Presentation of Philosophy and Its History

Ulrich Steinvorth

A Brief Presentation of Philosophy and Its History

Two Basic Questions

palgrave
macmillan

Ulrich Steinvorth
University of Hamburg
Hamburg, Hamburg, Germany

ISBN 978-3-031-72532-6   ISBN 978-3-031-72533-3   (eBook)
https://doi.org/10.1007/978-3-031-72533-3

This Palgrave Macmillan imprint is published by the registered company Springer Nature Switzerland AG.
The registered company address is: Gewerbestrasse 11, 6330 Cham, Switzerland

If disposing of this product, please recycle the paper.

CONTENTS

CHAPTER 1

What This Essay Aims at

Abstract This book showcases philosophy for people with little time. Therefore, it's very short, like Thomas Nagel's *Very Short Introduction to Philosophy* (1987). Nagel, though, presents only questions discussed at his time in philosophy seminars in the Western world. He doesn't introduce to the philosophy that once was a historical factor, that was hated and died for, that split into schools of which the two most important ones are fighting still today, the party that claims to be true philosophy, led by Plato, and the party led by Protagoras, today known as ideology. Nagel doesn't mention ideology, nor any philosopher's name.

To focus on history in a short introduction risks bias. What do you pick out? I scan history by following two questions that are widely considered typically philosophical, metaphysical, and the *ultimate* question*s*: *What does it all mean?* and *What is real rather than illusionary?* The *meaning question* was used by Nagel as the first title of his *Very Short Introduction*; I'm not alone in judging this question basic for philosophy. The *reality question* is no less basic; it precedes the meaning question, historically and logically. Note that moral philosophy and aesthetics don't seem to ask one of these questions; so, I'll have to argue why they are philosophical, regardless.

Keywords Introduction to philosophy • Metaphysical questions • The meaning question • The reality question

Philosophy was a passion for those who started it; its adepts gave their life for it. Thales was mocked, Anaxagoras expelled, Socrates killed. Today, it's a job with a sinking repute, but spreading in schools. Philosophers attacked each other for betraying philosophy and founded communities and academies to keep it clean. The most important ancient conflict lives on. Protagoras, a sophist who considered himself also a philosopher, declared in his *homo mensura* thesis man the measure of all things: what majorities or the ruling few judge to be true *is* true. Plato was upset; philosophy, he said, discovers universal truths, obliging everyone, as Socrates had shown. Yet the comedian Aristophanes and most Athenians considered Socrates a sophist as condemnable as Protagoras. Today, again the ideologists argue truth is what people, necessitated by laws of nature and history, think is true; philosophers claim they are not ideologists, and non-philosophers cannot tell philosophy from ideology. Yet philosophy is accepted, ideology condemned, as were the sophists. Ideology alone inherited the properties that once also made philosophy disliked. But why? Protagoras' *homo mensura* is compatible with the rule of majorities and democracy, while Plato, an aristocrat, claiming that reality rather than man decides on truth and justice, was an enemy of democracy.

Philosophy needs explanation, if only because everyone should know what is spreading in schools though losing reputation. The conflict between Protagoras and Plato shows there are two ways to understand philosophy: as opinion making by the power of words rather than the power of weapons and as discovering truths comparable to and obliging like mathematics. Ideologists but also philosophers follow the first way, Plato and other philosophical critics of ideology, the second. For the first, knowledge is the opinion held by mankind or its majority or rulers; for the latter, knowledge is the result of exploring reality the way mathematics does.

For reasons I'll explain later I follow Plato's claim that knowledge is independent of majority opinions. This has considerable political consequences (Steinvorth 2023) and requires revising philosophy's self-understanding. Yet while Plato assumed that what makes philosophy knowledge is the knowledge of *ideas* that he became famous for, I'll only assume there are two questions answering which makes philosophy as independent of majorities as mathematics, questions by which we can define philosophy. Non-philosophers consider these questions typically philosophical and rate them as *ultimate questions*: *What does it all mean?* and *What is real rather than illusionary?*

Thomas Nagel, in his *Very Short Introduction to Philosophy* (1987), whose shortness is the model for this presentation's brevity, used the first question as its first title; I call it the *meaning question*. Yet I distinguish from it the second that I call the *reality question*. It asks how *reality*, being, meaning, or truth differs from illusion, non-being, nonsense, or falsity. I assume these questions are, first, generally considered *metaphysical*, second, *fundamental* in the sense that they concern everything; for we can ask of anything what it means and whether it is real. I don't consider them *eternal*, the same at all ages, for I assume that in the history of philosophy their meaning has changed and that we must take this change into account to understand philosophy. Yet by the latter assumption I deviate from the prevalent non-historical approach to philosophy, brilliantly presented by Nagel's *Very Short Introduction*. Nagel also declares the "center of philosophy lies in certain questions which the reflective human mind finds naturally puzzling ... the best way to begin the study of philosophy is to think about them directly" (1987: 3). But to think about philosophical questions "directly" means to think about them regardless of historical facts. He manages to write an introduction to philosophy without mentioning any philosopher. This is success, as philosophy *is* asking certain questions rather than knowing what philosophers have said. But he doesn't introduce to its history, and this is a momentous downside.

For he doesn't introduce to the philosophy that was hated, changed history, and may have bequeathed its power to change the world to ideology—of which there is no word in Nagel's *Introduction*. Philosophy's history is important because we can't fully understand philosophical problems without knowing *their* history. We should know what earlier answers achieved, whether and why they failed, and what is the role and relation of ideology to philosophy.

Yet presenting philosophy as the history of answers to the meaning and the reality questions faces the difficulty that an established way to divide philosophy is that into theoretical, practical, and aesthetic philosophy. Presenting philosophy by the two questions implies that *theoretical philosophy* answers the reality question and *practical and aesthetic philosophy* answers the meaning question. The first implication is plausible, the second isn't. For practical and aesthetic philosophy analyze their problems regardless of the meaning question. I argue they *can* be understood as answering the meaning question and *must* be if we stick to the idea that also practical and aesthetic philosophy are *fundamental,* that is, ask questions applicable to everything, and I suggest we *should* stick to this idea.

Thus, the definition of philosophy that I imply by presenting it as asking the two questions turns out to be what you may have expected: *persuasive*. It *wants* the defined to be understood the way it is defined. Indeed, my presentation of philosophy is to show that philosophy was understood the way I want it to be understood, as asking the two fundamental questions with the effect, not necessarily intended, that the answers changed individuals and societies and could become guides to politics. To show that philosophy was thus understood is my *first aim*.

My claim that philosophy was thus understood is a hypothesis that is falsified if the history of philosophy can be better understood by another hypothesis. But a short presentation cannot discuss alternative ways to understand philosophy's history; it can only point to conspicuous properties of the history of philosophy and what it may have influenced that become understandable by my hypothesis. So, my *second aim* is to show that my hypothesis can plausibly explain the course of the history of philosophy in the West and those aspects of society that are likely influenced by philosophy. I claim to tell *a* true story of Western philosophy rather than *the* true story.

I point out that ancient Greece conceived science as the judge to answer the reality question, and that in the seventeenth century, science was generally recognized as this judge. Thus, philosophy suffered a dramatic loss of importance. The loss became nearly fatal when a century later, Enlightenment passed the meaning question to faith, which meant, to the private decisions of individuals that cannot claim universal validity. I present philosophy's history as a near suicide that philosophy escaped only because some questions proved unanswerable by science and faith.

I also show that the near suicide was a catastrophe. Passing the meaning question to faith, Enlightenment allowed ideologies to answer the meaning question and to set goals that caused conceptual and mental confusion, wars, and moral disaster. The catastrophe was a tragedy, as it was triggered by mistakes comparable to Aristotle's *hamartia,* the small venial weakness that leads to disaster. Philosophy, as the Enlightenment insisted, cannot tell us *the* meaning of life, but it can, as the ideologists claimed, say something universally valid about the meaning, though only by stating obliging *acceptance conditions* for answering the meaning question, the most important of which is, I claim, that such answers must conform to what science can accept as *value progress.* Yet calling philosophy's history a tragedy implies that philosophy is corrigible, for presenting a tragedy allows the public to change their life.

So, my *third aim* is to show that philosophy is a corrigible tragedy. To show that science can tell us something important about value progress, hence about the meaning of life, I discuss in two chapters Weber's sociology.

I also have a *formal* aim. I want to attain my three aims in a presentation as short as Nagel's *Introduction*. People curious about philosophy but short of time should find what now they cannot, a small book that like a good map makes them street-smart, able to locate their own and other people's standpoint and to understand why philosophy doesn't want to be ideology. Short presentations can stick in memory but risk falsity, or they are impeccable but deadly dull. I opted for the first way, hoping it presents truth. It's up to the non-philosophers to say whether this presentation clicks, and to the second part of my hoped-for readers, the philosophical experts and their colleagues: political theorists, historians, theologians, sociologists, scientists, art critics, and artists, to judge if it is true.

LITERATURE

Nagel, Thomas. "What is it like to be a bat?" In Mortal Questions. New York: Cambridge UP. *What Does it All Mean? A Very Short Introduction to Philosophy*. New York: Oxford UP 1987

Steinvorth, Ulrich. "Zur Legitimität des Klonens." In Ludger Schwarte, Hg., Körper und Recht: anthropologische Dimensionen der Rechtsphilosophie. München: Fink. *Unterdrückung durch Beglückung. Eine liberale Revision der politischen Philosophie*. Hamburg: Meiner 2023

CHAPTER 2

The Reality Question, Science, or From Thales to Aristotle

Abstract Ancient Greek philosophy answers the reality question, though the meaning question loomed. It raised doubts about the reality of gods and the existence of the perceptible empirical world, fascinating the few and appalling the many who wouldn't shrink from condemning Socrates to death. Philosophers, too, felt obliged to distinguish between philosophical achievements and bullshit, trying to relieve the reality question of its weirdness. Most important among them was Aristotle. His *Categories* reinforces a trend of ancient Greek philosophy to become what today we call science.

The Milesian school of Thales, Anaximander, and Anaximenes probably introduced the concept of a *substrate* of nature that stays the same in the changes of nature. Parmenides appealed to reason as the only reliable judge of what there is and concluded it must be perfect and unchangeable, as else, it wouldn't be perfect. Hence anything perceptible, as it is everchanging, is an illusion.

Plato follows Parmenides' degradation of the perceptible but grants the perceptible the status of partaking in the unchangeable perfect being, which he conceives as unchangeable patterns of virtues and mathematical objects, calling them *ideas*. Aristotle escapes the difficulties of Plato's concept of partaking by conceiving being as *binary*, that is, either existing or not existing, without the possibility that something exists only to a degree, and therefore lacking any value that things have in Plato's view, depending

U. Steinvorth, *A Brief Presentation of Philosophy and Its History*,
https://doi.org/10.1007/978-3-031-72533-3_2

on how far they partake in the perfection of ideas. Aristotle's concept has become that of modern science.

Keywords The reality question • Science • Categories • The substrate • Perfect being • Methexis • Binary

Philosophy is both attractive and repellent because its two questions are weird and the weird attracts and repels. Its weirdness distinguishes its questions from practical problems that demand clearing an obstacle without resetting the action courses. Philosophy requires rethinking the plots. The meaning question looks less weird than the reality question; as today philosophers are eager to show their ordinariness, Nagel could introduce philosophy by the meaning question. Yet the reality question, too, constitutes philosophy. Though there are ordinary ways to decide if something we face is real rather than an illusion, such as pricking one's arm or remembering what one has done some time ago, everyone understands when poets say life is a dream (Calderon 1636) or Descartes (1996 [1641]) imagines that the world we know including our ways to make sure we are not dreaming is but the work of an evil god who has us believe what is false. More recent philosophers *imagined we are* brains in a vat and our lives are the hallucinations of neurons stimulated by a super-intelligence (Putnam 1981). Such doubts express the reality question; they still attract—Elon Musk (2018) followed them in the form that a super-intelligence produces our lives as a computer simulation (Bostrom 2003)—and repel, as Musk (2018) got a lot of guffaws. Calderon's doubts, too, live on, though in a less beautiful form, in Kafka's (1915) nightmare that our life is that of a cockroach and in Huxley's (1932) suspicion that life in modern societies is a collective illusion.

Greek philosophy started with the reality question, though the meaning question loomed. It raised doubts about the reality of gods and the existence of the empirical world, delighting a minority and appalling the majority that condemned Socrates to death. Philosophers, too, felt obliged to distinguish between philosophical achievements and nonsense, trying to relieve the reality question of its weirdness. The most important among them was Aristotle. He reinforced a trend that moved Greek philosophy from its beginning in the early sixth century BC, its trend to become what today we call science—as far as we can guess, because our knowledge of the beginning of Greek philosophy is filtered by Aristotle and Plato, our main sources of knowing about it.

Thales of Miletus (~624-~545), mocked for his falling in a well when observing the sky, but admired for making money when he wanted to, his student Anaximander, and Anaximander's student Anaximenes, looked for the substance of the universe that was to guarantee true being (K&R Ch. II ff). To use the Aristotelian term of the Neoplatonist and Aristotle commentator Simplicius (c. 480–560), the Milesians looked for the *substrate* (*hypokeimenon*) to whatever happens. Anaximander said it is the *apeiron*, the limitless or indefinite (K&R 108f), and described it as that "from which come into being all the heavens and the worlds in them", adding that "the source of coming-to-be for existing things is that into which destruction, too, happens" (K&R 106f). This description, one of the rare fragments of early Greek philosophy preserving the original words, seems to have impressed contemporaries for its solemnity.

Anaximander's teacher Thales and student Anaximenes were soberer. The former said the substrate was water, the latter, air. All of them called the substrate divine (K&R 94,114,150); by modern concepts, they were pantheists rather than scientists. They identified true being with the divine, but also the divine with the substrate. The substrate changed from an object of awe and veneration into one of argument and analysis, the forms of science.

Yet how do argument and analysis tell truth and reality from falsity and illusion? This question gains center stage in Parmenides, at least a generation younger than Anaximenes. He proclaimed *reason, nous,* to be the judge to distinguish between true and false, becoming the ancestor of the appeals to reason that abound in the modern age, and ascribed to reason the character of a divine perfect being that doesn't deceive. But as a result, he rejected the Milesians' beginning of science. For reason, he argued, tells us that the divine is not only unperishable, as the Milesians implied by their concept of a world substrate, but also perfect. Being perfect, it must be unchangeable, for by a change the perfect can only become more perfect or less perfect, so neither way it would be perfect, so it must be unchangeable. Hence, the divine cannot be something from which everything arises and into which it decays; it must be unchangeable, and perception, showing us that the world is changing, is an illusion.

Parmenides' student Zeno construed paradoxes to prove that logically, that is, for reason, change is impossible. The best known of his paradoxes is that of swift-footed Achilles unable to overtake a tortoise, because whenever he moves closer, the tortoise has also moved, small though its progress has been. Parmenides must have loved paradoxes too, for he compared being—true reality—with a perfectly round unchangeable and timeless ball. His answer to the reality question is obviously weird, but as clear as philosophy should be. Reality, being or existence, which he didn't distinguish, is perfect and unchangeable. The ever-changing perceptible world, hence, time, are illusions. How could anyone believe this? Well, if time is an illusion, so is our perishability.

Plato and Aristotle retained Parmenides' idea of the divine as unchangeable. Yet even Plato, who admired Parmenides, declared the perceptible to be real, though only as far as it *partakes* in the perfect being. But his concept of *partaking, methexis,* implies two problems. First, there must be something imperfect and without value to partake in the perfect and its value. Plato recognizes this condition in his *Timaeus,* declaring that in addition to the perfect being and the perceptible partaking in it, there must be a third type, a *tritos genos,* "the receptacle (or nurse, if you like) of all creation" (49a). It was understood as space or matter. Plato argues it is not *being* but *becoming.* This argument is less fishy than it seems, as we still don't know what space or matter is (in the seventeenth century, it was even argued it was God, Koyré 1957/1968: 150f). But it set a bad model for verbal maneuvering not to admit an error.

The second problem of Plato's *methexis* is that for something perceptible to be, it partakes in the perfect *more or less*; it *is* to the degree it partakes; its being is gradable. But in ordinary thinking, something either is or isn't, *tertium non datur*: there is nothing gradable in being, being is a binary concept. So, Aristotle could well consider being or reality to be just what Plato said it was not: something without value and binary, like Plato's *tritos genos.* To be, things needn't participate in something perfect, they just are value-free and binary. They can become perfect, but for something to be, it needn't partake in perfect being, which, hence, isn't true being.

As Marx turned his teacher upside down, so did Aristotle. Hegel conceived reality as the evolution of mind, *Geist,* and individuals as its attributes. Plato conceived it as the perfect being and individuals as something partaking in it. Aristotle and Marx turned what their masters considered attributes into substances. But Aristotle didn't deny divine perfect being. He shrank it to the existence of gods who cause all movement but are not the source of being, as the divine is for Plato. Yet the depth of his deviation from Plato was obvious. In Miletus, Thales seems to have taught that it is the greatest honor to the master if his pupils differ from him by argument.

Hence, the amazing succession of theories claiming the substrate is water, *apeiron*, and air. In Plato's Academy, Aristotle felt obliged to declare, before listing his arguments for his reality conception, that it is more important for a philosopher to follow his arguments rather than friendship (NE 1, 1096a14-29)—friendship to his teacher Plato that it seems he lost.

Aristotle's main reason for differing from Plato was not respect for ordinary language, but that he saw himself as a natural scientist, a *physikos*, who wanted to examine the objects that Parmenides had declared an illusion. Probably to show how perceptible things can be the object of science (Spangler 1979: 92), he wrote his *Categories*. This text is considered the beginning of his metaphysics (cp. Frede 1987), containing his first answer to the reality question and telling us how to describe phenomena of nature. It lists ten classes of predicates or "predicables", called by Aristotelians *categories*, distinguishes between the first category as subject and the rest as its predicates, determines the subject as *ousia*, most often translated as *substance*, and says that substances are individuals such as Socrates or a horse, and their species, the class of humans or horses.

As to the categories that he lists in addition to (1) substances—(2) *quantities*, such as the weight of a substance, (3) *qualities*, such as its color, (4) *relations*, such as being bigger or smaller, (5) *place*, (6) *time*, (7) *position*, whether it is sitting or lying, (8) *having*, such as whether it has shoes on or an armor, (9) how it acts, whether it burns or cuts, and (10) how it is acted on, whether it can be burnt or cut (*Categories* Chap. 4)— we may wonder why he lists *position* and *having* as predicables, as they seem reducible to other predicables (Moravcszik 1967: 144). Yet the list tells us under which heads to examine nature and to make sure we deal with reality rather than illusion. So, the text could become a bible for empirical science. With the success of modern physics it lost renown, because Plato's concept of being proved more congenial to the scientists' goal of discovering laws than Aristotle's empiricism.

In the twentieth century, Aristotle's *Categories* and consequently his metaphysics were even more radically criticized. This criticism is worth considering as it can clarify Aristotle's arguments and show the importance of *propositional languages* that I'll explain in Chap. 6. Fritz Mauthner, at his time influential in linguistics, claimed: "If Aristotle had spoken Chinese or Dakota, necessarily he would have arrived at an entirely different logic, or at least an entirely different category doctrine" (2019, vol. 3, Erster Teil I, beginning). Linguists, appealing to Edward Sapir and Lee Whorf, raised similar objections. However, they didn't distinguish between two claims of the *Categories*, its *structure thesis* and its *substance thesis*. The first tells us something about human language: that it structures the world into substance and attributes; the second tells us something about the world: what substances are.

The structure thesis is true because all humans speak a *propositional language*. Unlike *signal* languages, propositional languages distinguish between cries or commands and descriptions. By their descriptions, they structure reality into a substrate or substance A and its attributes B. But A needn't be an Aristotelian substance (individual or species), it may be an all-comprehensive process of nature or stream of consciousness. Hence, Aristotle's structure thesis doesn't imply his substance thesis. Lichtenberg was right to criticize Descartes for inferring from the existence of thinking (*"es denkt, there is thinking"*) the existence of a thinking subject (1991: 412; similarly, Nietzsche 1980, vol. 11: 69f). Yet Aristotle's *Categories* do not imply that the structure thesis implies the substance thesis; so the substance of my thinking may be an all-comprehensive process rather than me.

Science does use Aristotle's reality concept, but this concept doesn't imply his substance thesis either. Science might use Plato's concept of reality as partaking in the perfect being and yet claim that individuals and species are substances. For science allows conceiving reality as an all-comprehensive process starting with the Big Bang, with individuals being determined by this process, as determinists claim, rejecting Aristotle's substance thesis. But even in this conception, science understands the all-comprehensive process as binary and value-free. So, science uses Aristotle's concept of being, but hasn't yet decided whether the substance of the world are individuals or an all-comprehensive process.

LITERATURE

Bostrom, Nick. "Are you living in a computer simulation?" *Philosophical Quarterly* 53, 2003, 243–55

Calderon de la Barca, Pedro. *La vida es sueño (Life is a dream)* Madrid 1636

Descartes, René. *Meditations on First Philosophy: With Selections from the Objections and Replies*, Cambridge: Cambridge UP, tr. Cottingham, 1996

Frede, Michael. *Essays in Ancient Philosophy*, University of Minnesota Press, Minneapolis, 1987

Huxley, Aldous. *Brave new World*, London: Chatto and Windus 1932

Kafka, Franz. "Die Verwandlung". *Die weißen Blätter*, ed. René Schickele. Oct. 1915

Koyré, Alexandre. *From the Closed World to the Infinite Universe*, Baltimore: John Hopkins Pr. 1957

Lichtenberg, Georg Christoph. *Schriften und Briefe*. Bd. 2. München: Hanser 1991

Mauthner, Fritz. *Beiträge zu einer Kritik der Sprache* (1913), Leipzig: Librorium Editions 2019, Bd. 3

Moravcszik, John. "Aristotle's Theory of Categories", in J.M. ed., *Aristotle. A Collection of Critical Essays*, New York 1967, 125–45

Musk, Elon. https://www.youtube.com/watch?v=xBKRuI2zHp0-   2018. Obtained Oct. 11, 2023

Nietzsche, Friedrich. *Sämtliche Werke*. Kritische Studienausgabe. München: dtv 1980

Putnam, Hilary. *Reason, Truth, and History*. New York: Cambridge UP 1981

Spangler, O. A. "Aristotle's Criticism of Parmenides in Physics I". *Apeiron*, 13(2), 1979, 92–103, 92

CHAPTER 3

Plato, or the Inebriant Answer to the Reality Question

Abstract Aristotle's concept of being prevailed, but Plato's concept remained attractive. It implies that the perceptible has value and meaning by partaking in the perfection of ideas and thus explains the worth of things in nature that many people believe in. Still more important, as to the ideas belong mathematical principles, perceptible nature partakes in mathematical principles, setting science the task of discovering mathematical laws that a divine architect might have used when constructing the perceptible and ever-changing world.

In contrast, Aristotle's concept seems to imply that nature is meaningless, which Aristotle disliked. Hence, he ascribes *tele*, innate goals, to the things of nature, allowing him to claim that nothing in nature is in vain or meaningless. This claim looks like an addition that doesn't fit in with his concept of a binary and valueless reality. But it reapproaches Plato's concept.

Keywords Being • Platonic ideas • Valueless • Meaningless • Teleology

Aristotle's answer to the reality question is sober: we understand the real as binary, value-free, and as substances that are individuals and their species. It did promote empirical science, but science became the basis of modern societies only when scientists listened to Plato's inebriant answer to the reality question.

Had Plato written a text comparable to the *Categories*, he would have declared the perfect being to be the substance, and individuals and their species, its attributes. He understood as the perfect being the being shared by *ideas*, which, with some plausibility, he had introduced in his early dialogues to explain how we can understand virtues and mathematical objects without experience. To call an empirical action just or an empirical figure circular, we must know, he argued, the non-empirical *idea* of justice and the *idea* of a circle. We cannot understand ideas either, he seems to have gone on arguing, without knowing their idea, the *idea of the ideas*. This idea is a necessary condition for anything not only to be *known* but also to *exist*. He called it *the idea of the good,* to emphasize the perfection of this topmost being, describing it as "beyond being and surpassing it by dignity and power" (Rep. 509b). Howsoever we understand this, Aristotle didn't even list anything normative in his *Categories.*

In his conflict with Plato, Aristotle could rely on ordinary language and the views of reality suggested by it. Plato relied on attractions of a reality conception no less powerful. Aristotle's *Categories* require us to check whether what claims to be real can be described in a statement whose logical subject can be analyzed as an individual or a species. Thus, when a cat dissolves but his grin remains, the phenomenon is an illusion. But philosophy's questions are weird, Plato takes account of this fact, while Aristotle represents philosophers' efforts to understand their problems as ordinary. Plato's referring existence and truth to a perfect being doesn't convince in ordinary situations. But think of the doubts about reality expressed by Calderon and Descartes, Kafka and Aldous Huxley. Can their doubts be dissolved in another way than by showing that we partake in something perfect? The feeling that what we do is shallow is a reason to doubt that we are in contact with true reality, while we are ready to take the kind of elation Plato describes when he describes contact with ideas a proof that we are in contact with what is *true being.*

In this defense of Plato's concept of being we can confirm that it is not enough to reject the Cartesian doubt of the reality of the world by pointing to the ordinary criteria by which to distinguish between dream and reality, such as pricking one's arm or checking a phenomenon by Aristotle's categories. Such criteria can only show that we go on living the life we lived before. But when we feel attracted to Plato's claim that reality is partaking in something perfect, the reality question that I assumed Greek philosophers wanted to answer changes into the meaning question. For perfection guarantees there is meaning in what we take for real. In contrast, Aristotle's claim that what is, just is, value-free though it can become valuable, sounds like the bleak contention that being is not only value-free but meaningless. Yet we don't want reality to be meaningless.

Aristotle, I think, saw that the bleak inference can be drawn from his *Categories*. To prevent it, he developed his *teleology*, his claim that every substance has a *telos*, an inbuilt goal it pursues by its nature. Earth and water, being heavy, sink; air and fire, being light, rise; the acorn's *telos* is the oak, and the oak's telos is the production of acorns. Aristotle's teleology presents nature as doing nothing in vain (Pol.1, 1253a6, Peri Poreias 704b11ff, 708a9ff), hence having meaning. Yet Aristotle explains *motion* not by the *tele* but by the divine, as things strive for the divine and matter that things are made of doesn't move by itself. He seems to use the divine only when he can't find a natural explanation: to answer why matter moves at all (*Metaph.* XII 6) and, probably, why reason can be "active" and "unmixed" with matter (*De An.* III 5). Compared to Plato's divine, Aristotle's divine is a *deus ex machina*, added to a world that doesn't need the divine but only *tele*, which are deducible from the nature of a thing.

The theater character of Aristotle's theology becomes obvious in his answer to the question of how many unmoved movers there might be. He thinks 47 movers are necessary to move the 47 spheres (that he believed encircle the earth), which bring motion into the cosmos (Met. 1073b1-74a17). This answer reminds readers today of the supercomputer's answer to "the Ultimate Question of Life, the Universe, and Everything" (Douglas Adams 1985): "*42*". It seems the scientist in Aristotle who explains things by their constitution and the believer in Zeus' divine power made a rotten compromise. The compromise brings Aristotle closer to Plato; already ancient Aristotle scholars like Porphyry emphasize his similarity to Plato (Chadwick 1986/2001: 19), and many modern scholars follow suit. But for philosophy's history, Aristotle is important as promoting the concept of reality as binary and value-free that risks presenting reality as meaningless.

Modern scientists reject explaining nature by *tele* or final causes, or teleology, but as little as Aristotle they believe that nature does anything in vain. Like Einstein, they believe that God doesn't dice, implying that nature has a meaning. But unlike Aristotle they found a way to make this belief compatible with the belief that reality is value-free. This way is the belief that the *laws* they look for prove that nature has a meaning, even if it is a meaning obvious only for the creator god. Science recognizes the divinity of nature by discovering its laws. This belief is a heritage from Plato's concept of reality as necessarily partaking in perfect being that Aristotle's *Categories* reject.

Plato's reality concept shaped not only the Jewish, Christian, and Muslim theology but also science. By insisting that there *is* anything only as far as it partakes in something perfect, Plato encouraged science in another but no less important way than Aristotle by insisting that things exist in a value-free and binary sense. For if reality is divine, the world is a perfect being's product that despite its imperfections must in one respect be as good as the perfect being it rises from: in the way it is built. Consequently, Plato speculates in his *Timaeus* about the perfect principles according to which the demiurge, the architect of the world, built it. Thus, Plato set science the task not just to collect empirical data but to explain them by laws, excluding their explanation by demonic or divine intervention, and by mathematical laws at that, because Plato, like most scientists, found perfection in mathematics.

Platonists looked for laws of a divine world architect, Aristotelian *physikoi* insisted on collecting empirical data, and yet they united in making what became science the judge on the reality question. An empirical fact confirmed their union. Aristotle had pointed to smooth shifts between genera and species: "nature passes little by little from inanimate beings to animals in such a way that, as a consequence of this continuity, one hardly notices the border between them nor to which of the two groups an intermediate form belongs" (*History of Animals* 8.1, 588b4; cp. *Parts of Animals* 4.5, 681a12; quotations from Pellegrin 2023: 117). Platonists considered the passages a result of perfect laws that nature partakes in, though only more or less, Aristotelians considered them an effect of *tele* to be empirically described in value-free and binary terms. Both parties found their concept of reality confirmed by the same biological facts but differed in their interpretation. How then could they unite in making science the judge on the reality question? To find an answer, we must look at how the Neoplatonist Plotinus interpreted the facts.

LITERATURE

Adams, Douglas. *The Hitchhiker's Guide to the Galaxy: The Original Radio Scripts.* London: Pan Books 1985

Chadwick, Henry. *Augustine: A Very Short Introduction.* New York: Oxford UP 1986/2001.

Pellegrin, Pierre. *Animals in the World. Five Essays on Aristotle's Biology,* Albany: SUNY Pr. 2023

CHAPTER 4

Plotinus, or the Meaning of the Meaning Question

Abstract Plotinus' theology anticipates Darwin's theory of evolution, though it reverses Darwin's development from the simple to the complex. Doesn't it anticipate modern science? It does presuppose a divine origin but that doesn't make it unscientific. For though modern science contributed to the disenchantment of the world, it wouldn't have arisen without Plato conceiving being as perfect and divine. Nor is it unscientific because Plotinus *values* evolution, preferring the complex. Modern biologists, too, consider the complex higher than the primitive, though Darwin forbad himself to think of the more complex as higher.

The reason we cannot accept Plotinus' theory as science is not that he finds meaning in nature but that he understands meaning as something imposed by a (divine) mind on meaningless facts. He doesn't allow things and facts to be *immanently* meaningful. But a sunset, say, may be meaningful without implying that behind it there is a mind that intends us to understand the meaning of the event. True, sometimes there is a mind behind something meaningful for us, say someone who wants us to understand a smile as the sign of happiness. But such an intention is possible only because certain movements and gestures have meaning for us regardless of someone's intention.

Science understands the meaning that it does discover, such as the natural evolution, like a sunset or an unintended smile. It takes any meaning it finds in nature for immanent, not for transcendent and a proof of the

U. Steinvorth, *A Brief Presentation of Philosophy and Its History*, https://doi.org/10.1007/978-3-031-72533-3_4

existence of a creator god who imposed his meaning on the world, as did Plotinus. Science doesn't deny that we might look for a transcendent meaning, but distinguishes itself from such an enterprise, which we may call theology, by limiting itself to immanent meaning. It is important to stick to immanent meaning. Otherwise, science would be theology.

Keywords Science • Evolution • Darwin • *causa sui* • Matter • Immanent and transcendent meaning

Plotinus (205–270, no Christian, but of influence on Augustine, Chadwick 1986/2001: 17ff) understood the passages between the natural species as their gradual partaking in the perfect being that he calls the One. The gradual partaking became popular as the *Great Chain of Being*, the *scala naturae, nature's ladder* (Lovejoy 1936). He assumed with Plato that the world was created by a "being devoid of envy, … he desired that everything should be so far as possible like himself" (Timaeus 29e). Yet the logic of omnipotence prevents the One from creating a flawless world. For the One has the unique quality of existing by its own power, being *causa sui, "aition heautou kai par' hautou kai di' hauton"*, the cause of itself and of all other things and operating through them (Enneads VI 14. 41; Summerell 2002.). If you ask how anything can be *its own cause*, take it as the quality of being uncreated but able to create. He explains the smooth passages in nature by the creation of a power that because of its omnibenevolence creates and despite its omnipotence cannot prevent its creation from having evil things. His theory is both an explanation of facts, like science, and a justification of God, a theodicy.

In a first "emanation", the One creates creatures as powerful in intelligence and will as itself. Yet necessarily, they are created and no *causa sui*. Plotinus doesn't mention the legends of a fall of angels rebelling against God but implies them. The logical impossibility for the most perfect creations to be *causa sui* is a reason for them to grudge the One its uniqueness (explicated by Kierkegaard, cp. Steinvorth 2020: 166f, and expressed by Lautréamont saying, "My subjectivity and a creator, this is too much for my brain", cp. Camus 1951: 111; my tr.). Christian theology ascribing to the Almighty a son, sharing with him eternal existence but being sired, evades an answer to the problem.

Plotinus also presents the *material* world as the result of the perfect goodness of the One, propagating itself not only in its form of spirit but also in matter. Whether he conceives matter as something the One creates out of nothing, as the Abrahamic religions teach, or in another way, he conceives matter as a lack of being that prevents creations in matter from perfection, the more so the more a creature is made of matter.

As a theologian, Plotinus is of greatest influence on Christian, Muslim, and Jewish theology and on philosophers such as Leibniz (Emilsson 2013) and Hegel (Wladika 2015). By presenting the world as a unique creation of the One, he implies a break with the ancient view of the world and time as circular, as the uniqueness of the creation rules out the former view of time. His theodicy is a paradigm of an answer to the meaning question, explaining how there can be meaning in a world that has evils. It is *meta-physics*, as in contrast to physics, it makes a claim on the meaning of facts. But it also anticipates Darwin's theory of evolution. Hence, is it also anticipating science?

We can understand the One as the creative power that determines nature, and the perfection in which creatures partake as the ability to act and respond in a most differentiated and creative way to stimuli. The least perfect creatures such as stones respond only to physical forces, while the more perfect creatures respond in a more differentiated and increasingly creative way. Darwin agrees with Plotinus that the natural species are products of the same force of nature in a process that explains the smooth transitions between them but differs by claiming that the chain of creatures ascends from imperfection to perfection. Yet Plotinus can argue that evolution is possible only if even the simplest form of being has or partakes in a power that enables it to evolve into the most prefect forms. Thus, isn't Plotinus a forerunner of modern science?

True, unlike modern science Plotinus ascribes meaning to evolution, as he understands it as a series of emanations of the One. But that a scientific theory ascribes meaning to the world doesn't disqualify it from science. On the contrary, modern science was possible only because it followed Plato's non-empiricist approach to look for mathematical laws by which to explain and predict events in nature. This approach presumes that it belongs to the meaning of the world that it can be explained by laws that a most intelligent world architect, Plato's *demiurge,* has used and will not intervene in. This is a metaphysical claim that all modern science presupposes, as it bans explanation by divine or demonic intervention (on this, cp. Smart 2003: 46 and Wittgenstein 1979). Banning divine intervention, science did push the *disenchantment* that viewed nature as accidental and meaningless (Weber WG 308). But it did because it excludes not meaning but divine intervention. Hence, that Plotinus anticipates science cannot be denied for the reason that he considers evolution and the creation of the world as a meaningful process.

And yet, Plotinus' claim that the world results from a necessary perfect being isn't scientific. For two reasons. First, his inverting evolution from an ascent into a descent implies incoherent assumptions on *matter* that disqualify it as science. When Plotinus says the One creates man and the lower members of the great chain of being *in matter*, he prompts the questions what he understands by *matter* and how he can assume that the One wants to reproduce himself not only in what he is himself, *spirit*. Does matter somehow exist when the One creates material creatures? But then matter would also be *causa sui* and the One wouldn't be the only one *causa sui* and not *the One*. Or does the One create matter along with the material creatures? But why then does he create a medium which brings in so many evils, mortality, malformation, disease, unreliability, crime? Or is matter just nothing and any material creation necessarily a creation into nothing, necessarily burdened with evils? What then is left of the One's omnipotence, and how can Plotinus have the One create the perfect angels? Science evades these incoherencies by conceiving being, since Aristotle, as something value-free and binary, as which we can also conceive matter. Plotinus cannot evade them and therefore cannot be recognized as anticipating science.

Second, his claim isn't scientific because he understood the meaning he found in nature as the effect of a divine mind who gave meaning to facts, rather than assuming that the meaning might belong to the fact and is *immanent*. For there are facts that have a meaning though no mind has given them meaning. Thus, smiles and frowns, blushing and blanching, opening one's hands and clenching one's fist, most of our and animals' unintended motions have an immanent meaning. We can intend to show someone our sympathy by smiling only because smiling has the intention-independent meaning of showing good will. Probably we also can intend anything only because there are behaviors with intention-independent meaning that we can learn to intend. In evolution, intention-independent meaningful behaviors precede intended actions. True, smilings and frownings have intention-independent meanings only *for* a mind *to* whom they have meaning. This is important because when we ask the meaning question, we ask what things mean *to us*, what they tell *us*. But this doesn't imply that there is a mind *by* whom they have meaning. Nature needs no god to have meaning. Plotinus but also later theorists miss this point.

When modern cosmology discovered that life and man would not have arisen if some constants of nature had only a slightly different value, physicists like Fred Hoyle found in this fact proof of nature's divine origin, as this fact could not be declared meaningless (Steinvorth 2013: 126ff). Hoyle was right to see meaning in this fact but like Plotinus wrong to see in meaningful facts proof of a Creator's working. Nor does nature lose meaning if evolution is a result of the forces of nature hitting accidentally the constants that allowed for our evolution in the billions of years since the Big Bang or in the infinity of time assumed if the Big Bang is one among an infinity of starting points of a universe. Howsoever we explain the cosmos, it is something to wonder about and to ask for its meaning. Such meaning doesn't presuppose a divine subject imposing its meaning on meaningless facts.

Moreover, the belief that there is no meaning in nature unless there is a mind that has given or created meaning by its will biases both science and theology. Hume was considered an atheist, as he (posthumously) called nature "contemptible" and "blind..., impregnated by a great vivifying principle, and pouring forth from her lap, without discernment or parental care, her maimed and abortive children" (1748/1948: 79). Since then, nature's scores went down to the low degrees it had gotten from the Gnostics in the early centuries AD. Thus Tennyson, Darwin's contemporary, found in evolution "nature, red in tooth and claw" (*In memoriam A.H.H.* 1850, canto 56).

Science could arise because scientists believed in a creator god building the world on laws he doesn't interfere with. It doesn't forbid assuming immanent meaning, nor philosophy asking the meaning question. It does forbid philosophy to assume transcendent meaning unless philosophy adduces positive evidence for transcendent meaning. However, Plotinus didn't adduce it. He thought that the smooth passages between the species indicated a chain of being that allows us to extrapolate a supernatural perfect being that must have emanated not only its being but also its meaning, importance, and value to decreasingly less perfect beings.

This was an error, but one he shared with many theorists. Not only Hoyle, but also Darwin fell victim to it when he forbad himself to talk of "higher" and "lower", believing such talk implies that a divine author had given the more complex species the meaning of being better than the less complex. As the biologist Ernst Mayr remarked, "Of course, Darwin did not follow his own advice" (1982: 530; cp. 1991: 64), adding:

> who can deny that overall there is an advance from the prokaryotes that dominated the living world more than three billion years ago to the eukaryotes ... from the single-celled eukaryotes to plants and animals ... from types with a small brain and low social organization to those with a very large central nervous system, highly developed parental care, and the capacity to transmit information from generation to generation? (1991: 62)

Who can deny, we may go on asking, that biological facts have the meaning of being an "advance", whether it is accidental or not? We can talk of *higher* or *lower* regardless of whether there was a god to intend it. Both Darwin and the declared atheist Dawkins (2017), who insists that evolution is accidental and *therefore* meaningless, presuppose the false premise that there is no meaning without a mind that imposes it on meaningless facts by its will.

So, we must understand the philosophical meaning question as asking what the *facts* tell us rather than what a god meant the facts to be. But asking for the meaning of facts implies value judgments as answers, for ascribing a meaning to a fact implies that the fact has a positive or negative value. Hence, was Hume wrong to claim we cannot deduce norms from facts (1740, III 1,1), and Moore to call such a deduction *naturalistic fallacy* (1903/1962)? In fact, we have just seen that Hume calls nature, pondering its behavior, "contemptible". We may save him from contradicting his own prohibition by pointing to the difference between facts and their meaning: we cannot deduce norms from facts but only from meanings; Hume calling nature contemptible held the premise "Children ought to be cared for" and found it as a meaning of the facts of nature. Yet despite such a defense, if we can find immanent meaning in the facts, this does shake Hume's and Moore's dualism of facts and values.

Now, we can clarify how Aristotelian empiricists and Platonist law-conjecturers could unite in making science the judge on the reality question. They could because they could take the meaning of facts as immanent to the world; the Platonists found it in their obeying laws that even the world architect would not intervene in, and the Aristotelians found it in the *tele* working in substances. In contrast, modern scientists find meaning in facts only if a subject has imposed an intention on them. In this respect, Plotinus sides with modern scientists, but makes the facts a proof of God, while scientists, to exclude this use, deny the facts any meaning.

LITERATURE

Camus, Albert. *L'homme révolté*. Paris: Gallimard 1951

Chadwick, Henry. *Augustine: A Very Short Introduction*. New York: Oxford UP 1986/2001.

Dawkins, Richard. *Science in the Soul: Selected Writing of a Passionate Rationalist*. London: Bantam 2017

Emilsson, Eyjólfur Kjalar. "Leibniz, Plato, Plotinus." In Karfík, Filip and Euree Song, eds., *Plato Revived*. Berlin: de Gruyter, 2013

Hume, David. A Treatise of Human Nature, ed. Selby-Bigge and Nidditch, Oxford: Clarendon Press. *Dialogues Concerning Natural Religion* (1748). New York: Hafner 1948

Lovejoy, Arthur Oncken. *The Great Chain of Being: A Study of the History of an Idea*, Cambridge: Harvard UP 1936

Mayr, Ernst. *The Growth of Biological Thought. Diversity, Evolution, and Inheritance.* Cambridge/MA: Harvard UP 1982

Mayr, Ernst. The Growth of Biological Thought. Diversity, Evolution, and Inheritance. Cambridge/MA: Harvard UP. *One Long Argument. Charles Darwin and the Genesis of Modern Evolutionary Thought.* Cambridge/MA: Harvard UP 1991

Moore, G.E. *Principia Ethica*. Cambridge: Cambridge UP (1903), 1962

Smart, J.J.C., and Haldane, John. *Atheism and Theism*, Oxford: Blackwell 2003

Steinvorth, Ulrich. "Zur Legitimität des Klonens." In Ludger Schwarte, Hg., Körper und Recht: anthropologische Dimensionen der Rechtsphilosophie. München: Fink. *The Metaphysics of Modernity*, Milwaukee: Marquette UP 2013

Steinvorth, Ulrich. "Zur Legitimität des Klonens." In Ludger Schwarte, Hg., Körper und Recht: anthropologische Dimensionen der Rechtsphilosophie. München: Fink. *A Secular Absolute. How Modern Philosophy Discovered Authenticity.* Palgrave Macmillan, New York 2020

Summerell, O. F. "Self-Causality from Plotinus to Eckhart and from Descartes to Kant". *Quaestio 2*, 2002, 493–518

Wittgenstein, Ludwig. Tractatus logico-philosophicus. In Schriften. Frankfurt/M: Suhrkamp. *Wittgenstein's Lectures, Cambridge 1932–1933*, ed. A. Ambrose. Oxford: Blackwell 1979

Wladika, Michael. "Aspects of Hegel's Interpretation of Plotinus". *Hegel-Jahrbuch* 2015, 124–131

CHAPTER 5

How Far Science Replaced Philosophy, or Descartes vs. Hobbes

Abstract Seventeenth-century science became the generally recognized judge on the reality question, just as ancient Greek philosophers had hoped. But modern science explained nature by laws that unlike Aristotelian physics forbad any exception from them, leaving no place for explanation by free will, although it seems that by our will we can falsify any prediction made about our actions if we know the prediction. Philosophers split over defining the scope of science. The majority followed Descartes declaring that science can explain only the movement of *bodies*, not what is ruled by *thought*, *will*, and *judgment*, dividing the one substance Aristotle assumed into the two substances of matter and mind. A minority, the materialists or physicalists, today the overwhelming majority, followed Hobbes, declaring mental phenomena must be explained by the same laws that explain the movements of bodies, implying that thinking, judgment, and will are "epiphenomena" that lack the causal force to have an effect on the world.

Although there are philosophical arguments for and against free will, and philosophy can check scientific claims and propose questions that science should find an empirical way to answer, it is science rather than philosophy that has become the judge on what there is and must decide whether there is free will by experiment and looking for new empirical data.

U. Steinvorth, *A Brief Presentation of Philosophy and Its History*,
https://doi.org/10.1007/978-3-031-72533-3_5

Keywords Modern science • Laws of nature • Body and mind •
Responsibility • Epiphenomenalism • Cybernetics

Since the seventeenth century, science has become the judge on the reality
question, as it convinced by its surprising predictions and by promoting
technology that changed the world. It left philosophy with the meaning
question, which, with tragical outcome, the Enlightenment dismissed a
century later. Yet philosophy didn't die out. It focused on normative questions without referring them to the meaning question, and it went on
asking the reality question because science couldn't completely settle it.
Here is a rough survey of the problems modern science confronts philosophy with.

Modern science disenchanted the world, leaving no place for gods and
demons to intervene nor for man to make him a member of nature. Blaise
Pascal, more exactly his *libertin*, the seventeenth century free thinker
(anticipated by Kepler and in contrast to Giordano Bruno, Koyré
1957/1968: 61 and 39–54) said: "The eternal silence of these infinite
spaces terrifies me" (1995: 73). Nietzsche echoed him in the often-quoted
verse "The world—a gate to thousand deserts, mute and chill" (2005, vol.
11: 329; I couldn't identify the translator). But he ignored that Darwin
had rediscovered the smooth transitions between the species that Plotinus
had exploited for his theodicy. Modern nihilism, as Jonas (1952) showed,
has a basis in what science teaches about nature. In the nineteenth century,
science had changed and made the idea of man's standing lost in a blind
universe, hence nihilism, a bit comical. But Darwinian science, too, suggested a new form of theodicy, which was used by ideologists to base social
Darwinism. Science triggered a new form of theodicy called ideology (cp.
below Chaps. 8 and 9) and thus reopened the reality question.

Even more than by its infinite spaces, science frightened by its iron laws
that rule without exception and seem to make man an appendix to nature
without a will of his own. In Aristotle's physics laws are not iron, because
our matter prevents us from always obeying the laws of nature; laws only
hold for the universe as far as it is rational (Byrne 2018: 5, 34). This
accords with Aristotle's claim that we are responsible not if we act volun-
tarily (for animals and children who are not responsible can act volun-
tarily) but if we rationally choose after deliberation (which animals and
children aren't capable of; NE III 1–3). But in physics, what Aristotle
considered the source of our irrationality, materiality, was the source of

our liberty not to follow the laws. This is a paradox that modern physics is not burdened with. Yet by assuming iron laws, even laws created by a perfect creator, it implies a pre-determinism that allows deducing from the laws of nature and the description of the initial conditions of the universe (say, the Big Bang) all future states till the end of time. This required rethinking human responsibility.

Ancient belief in a divine predetermination of the world didn't weaken belief in our responsibility, incompatible though they are. Rather, it led ancient Greeks to write tragedies that move us still today. It made the Hebrews develop ideas of a god who punishes man for his disobedience and bets on man's free choice of following him, the good god, rather than Satan (Job 1, 6ff). It made them develop ideas of man's original sin and of salvation that shaped the mind and the history of the West. Moreover, all civilizations we know believe in human responsibility, as people everywhere are punished for evils they are thought to have caused by their choice, unlike cattle and children who are trained not to cause damage, but not deemed responsible.

Hence, modern science had another reason, in addition to the question of whether theodicies and ideologies present us with reality, to again ask the reality question: are a responsible self and free will real? The question is again fundamental, for if free will is an illusion, anything is, as we believe that anything is what a true judgment says it is, and we believe we need free will (or rational deliberation, Aristotle's source of responsibility) to judge what anything is.

Philosophers might have rejected modern science's claims on iron laws if it had not become obviously superior to ancient science. It combined observation of facts and their explanation by principles in ways unseen by Aristotle and Plato. It devised instruments to discover facts and contrived experiments to check their explanation by law. To confirm their astronomical theories scientists invented telescopes. To prove his counter-intuitive claim that light and heavy bodies fall equally fast, Galileo had balls of different weight roll down inclined levels to abstract from air resistance. This was obvious progress, and scientists' sophistication and creative invention didn't stop after Galileo.

At Galileo's time, philosophers reacted promptly to the challenge of science. They agreed that science tells reality from illusion but split over how to think and judge on thinking and judging. The majority, led by Descartes, considered them inexplicable by the causal laws of science and reserved it to the reflections of philosophers, leaving the rest, matter, to science. Aristotle's one substance of individuals and their species, whose being he had conceived as value-free and binary, became two substances, body and mind. The realm of matter was assigned to the rule of causal laws, that of mind to the rule of logic or reason, and causal and logical laws were considered to exclude each other. Yet responsibility requires the mind to act on the body, and it was to save responsibility from its dissolution in causal predetermination that the Cartesians separated mind from body. But now, mind's separation from the body forbad the very action of mind on matter that responsibility presupposes. Cartesians (though not Descartes) bit the bullet. Interaction between body and mind *is* an illusion, they said. Rather, there is, as Leibniz called it (*Monadology* 1991 [1714]), a *pre-established harmony*, created by God, between the causal chain of bodies and the logical chain of thoughts.

There has probably never been a philosophical doctrine as far away from commonsense as the doctrine of the pre-established harmony. Commonsense tells us that when I have a reason to do something, my will can cause my body to move accordingly, and that when my body is hurt, it can cause my will to do something. Body and mind seem to interact, which Cartesians yet denied. But the philosophers who responded to Galileo's science didn't believe that "philosophy is to question and understand very common ideas that all of us use every day without thinking about them", as Nagel describes philosophy's "main concern" (1987: 5). Like their Greek predecessors, they rather thought that philosophy is to understand very uncommon ideas that arise with the progress of our knowledge.

Cartesianism could become the dominating philosophy on the continent because it provided a new basis for the Platonist view on the special status of thinking and judging that made Plato a fierce critic of Protagoras (cp. below Chap. 6). A minority of philosophers, led by Hobbes (*Lev.* Part I) and today the overwhelming majority, rejected Descartes' splitting of Aristotelian monism and argued for "physicalism", the claim that the substance is matter evolving into the species we know today. Their most influential fraction declared consciousness to be an effect of excitations of certain organic tissue. As Aldous Huxley's grandfather Thomas Huxley (1898 [1874]) said, consciousness lacks the causal power of body movements; it's an "epiphenomenon", comparable to the whistle of a steam engine that indicates steam leaving the machine without having a causal effect on the machine. It claims the idea that by my conscious will, I, a responsible self, cause a body part to move, hence, free will, is an illusion.

That epiphenomenalism contradicts commonsense was no grave objection. Yet that it contradicts institutions of justice and education was, and still is today. The most popular theory that sticks to physicalism but claims not to offend justice and education institutions is currently what is called *compatibilism*. It argues that we are free if we are free to do what we want to. Anselm of Canterbury had called freedom of this kind *freedom of action* to distinguish it from *free will* or *freedom of will*, as it doesn't imply the freedom to choose one's wants (Ekenberg 2005). Freedom of action is compatible with determinism, as my wants can be predetermined; free will is not. Since Augustine (Frede 2011; Steinvorth 2020, Ch. 8) free will was understood as the ability to both do and not do the same action. This includes the power to determine one's wants. Compatibilism results from conceptual confusion (Albritton 1985; McKenna 2019). Hence, whether free will is real or an illusion is still a philosophical problem.

But this fact doesn't quash science's authority to tell reality from illusion. Science has decided on a couple of mental phenomena that they are explainable by the principles of natural science, hence real. It has decided that consciousness is explainable as a property of organisms that helps them cope with their environment. It hasn't yet explained *how* consciousness arises, but *that* it exists is scientifically recognized. We know consciousness from ourselves and can tell, with a little help from Wittgenstein's later philosophy and linguistics, when other people and some animals are conscious and what they feel and think. We learn *other* minds by behavioral cues and use the same descriptive words to express our *own* pains, as we are trained to replace screams with words the way we are trained to replace uncontrolled behavior (say, peeing) by controlled one, without using criteria. True, there are animals of whom we don't know whether they have a mind. Do the parts of a worm that our spade has cut, both parts squirming, feel pain? We don't know, but we may one day find in cells some stuff indicating or excluding pain in worms. Whether there are other minds and how we know them is no longer a philosophical question. Claims on the consciousness of animals and humans contribute to a system of predictions confirmed by experience.

Hence, also philosophers expect science to decide if free will is real or an illusion. Philosophy may help find the right way, but science decides if the way is viable. Yet philosophers today want to show that their questions fascinate and attract students to seminars. Disinterested in history that might tell them that their problems are no longer philosophical, they indulge in asking how consciousness can arise and how or whether we can know other minds' *qualia,* the feeling of a color or smell or sound. Yet these problems, if they are problems, are scientific. Current philosophers' interest in presenting consciousness as an attractive phenomenon makes them forget what we know about consciousness and that it is a property of living metabolic organisms, hence unattainable by artificial intelligence presently much discussed. Nagel (1974/1979) even argued we cannot know other minds, at least not what it is like to be a bat. I guess he has never seen an ill bat miserably slogging along in daylight. The question of what it is like to be a bat is not *fundamental,* it doesn't apply to every-thing. This point already shows it isn't philosophical.

Although there is an overwhelming mass of philosophical literature on free will and much of it helps recognize the problem and ways how to solve it, it is science that decides on the still philosophical problem whether free will is real or an illusion. When Benjamin Libet (1979) checked the brain waves of the so-called *readiness potential* of subjects measurable before they consciously decide, which they indicate by clicking a button, and found a rise of the potential some fragments of a second before they click the button, this result was rightly considered important. Libet's first conclusion was that the subjects' decisions were caused by the rise of the readiness potential. Later (1985) he conjectured we can veto impulses when they become conscious, just as the adherents of the power of nega-tion from Augustine to Descartes (see next chapter) and libertarians like Nozick (1981) assume. Still today, what Libet's and similar experiments might show is controversial (Haynes 2013; Schultze Kraft et al. 2015). But their inconclusiveness doesn't prove that science cannot decide whether free will is real. Rather, philosophical reflections on what we understand by the idea of free will are a necessary precondition of deciding whether free will is real, but the final decision depends on predictions of human actions that come true against expectations.

Judging and the thinking that precedes judging is what philosophy including ideology and sophistic consists of. But the subject of judging divided Plato and Protagoras and, since the French Revolution, philoso-phers and ideologists. Judging presupposes, if the Platonist tradition is right, a responsible self; if the Hobbesian tradition is, it is a motion explained by the same laws that explain billiard ball motions. Newtonian physics, the pride of the moderns that proved their superiority to the ancients, might have proved the special powers of judgments, as science is a work of judgment. But its successes when it was applied to technology, medicine, and the understanding of societies and individuals seemed to prove that we are as predetermined as billiard balls and to disprove Cartesian *pre-established harmony*. And yet we can predict it will be difficult for science to prove free will to be an illusion. For people can, if they know the predictions made on them, falsify them, just to show their free will is no illusion.

Cybernetics, I conjecture, will help decide the open question. Cybernetic systems, the object of cybernetics, are mechanisms and organisms that respond to an input and check their response by feedbacking it to the responding part of the system so the system can pursue a task built into it. A thermostat is a cybernetic system in which some part responds to the input of a wanted temperature and another part feedbacks the effects of the responses to the part responding to inputs, so the wanted temperature is attained. We can think of humans as complex cybernetic systems that like ballistic missiles can target moving goals and can even reset any task, regardless of the program that has built them. Such a system has free will and a responsible self if there is a *random generator*, corresponding to the power of negation or of blocking impulses, to exclude predetermination, and *a rule to choose* among the random-generated possible actions in a way that makes the choice *self-determined*. Interestingly, we find these two parts also in the reflections of Descartes and Kant on how to understand judgments and free will. But to decide whether free will is real, such a cybernetic system must be proved to be constructible.

Literature

Albritton, Rogers. "Freedom of Will and Freedom of Action". *Proceedings and Addresses of the American Philosophical Association*, 59, 1985, pp. 239–251

Byrne, Christopher. *Aristotle's Science of Matter and Motion*. Toronto: University of Toronto Pr. 2018

Ekenberg, Tomas. "Free Will and Free Action in Anselm of Canterbury". *History of Philosophy Quarterly* 22, 2005, pp. 301–318

Frede, Michael. Essays in Ancient Philosophy, University of Minnesota Press, Minneapolis. *A Free Will: Origins of the Notion in Ancient Thought*. Ed. A. A. Long. Oakland: Univ. of California Pr. 2011

Haynes, J-D. "Beyond Libet", in A. Clark, J. Kiverstein, T. Vierkant, Hg., *Decomposing the Will*, Oxford: Oxford University Press 2013

Huxley, Thomas Henry. "On the hypothesis that animals are automata, and its history". *Fortnightly Review* 22, 1874, pp. 555–580. Reprint in *Method and Results*: Essays by Thomas H. Huxley, New York: Appleton, 1898

Jonas, Hans. "Gnosis and Modern Nihilism", *Social Research* 19, 1952, 430–52

Koyré, Alexandre. *From the Closed World to the Infinite Universe,* Baltimore: John Hopkins Pr. 1957

Leibniz, Gottfried Wilhelm. *The Monadology* (1714). Tr. Nicholas Rescher. University of Pittsburgh Pr 1991

Libet, Benjamin. "Unconscious cerebral initiative and the role of conscious will in voluntary action". *The Behavioral and Brain Sciences* 8, 1985, 529–566

Libet, Benjamin; Wright, E. W.; Feinstein, B.; Pearl, D. K. "Subjective Referral of the Timing for a Conscious Sensory Experience". *Brain* 102, 1979, 191–22

McKenna, Michael, "Compatibilism", *Stanford Encyclopedia of Philosophy* 2019

Nagel, Thomas. "What is it like to be a bat?" In *Mortal Questions.* New York: Cambridge UP 1979, 165–180

Nagel, Thomas. "What is it like to be a bat?" In Mortal Questions. New York: Cambridge UP. *What Does it All Mean? A Very Short Introduction to Philosophy.* New York: Oxford UP 1987

Nozick, Robert. *Philosophical Explanations.* Clarendon Press, Oxford 1981

Pascal, Blaise. *Pensées and Other Writings,* ed. Levi. Oxford: Oxford UP 1995

Russell, Bertrand. *In Praise of Idleness and Other Essays* (1935). London: Routledge 2005

Schultze-Kraft, M., … Haynes, J.-D. "The point of no return in vetoing self-initiated movements". *Proceedings of the National Academy of Sciences,* 113(4), 2015, 1080–1085

Steinvorth, Ulrich. "Zur Legitimität des Klonens." In Ludger Schwarte, Hg., Körper und Recht: anthropologische Dimensionen der Rechtsphilosophie. München: Fink. *A Secular Absolute. How Modern Philosophy Discovered Authenticity.* Palgrave Macmillan, New York 2020

CHAPTER 6

Propositional Language and the Power of Negation, or Kant and Descartes

Abstract Physicalism was unable to disqualify belief in free will because we seem to be able to reject inclinations if we deliberate them. This reasoning was first used by Aristotle and the Stoics to claim that adults capable of deliberation are responsible for actions they might have deliberated. The Stoics distinguished between understanding a thought and approving or rejecting it, and claimed that by our power of saying yes or no to a thought the *ego* becomes independent even of Zeus. Yet they shrank back from identifying this power with free will, as did Augustine. Descartes and Kant follow the same idea of judging as the Stoics, but Kant argues that the power of negation, which is the liberty of indifference, is not yet free will, claiming that we get the idea of free will only in our experience that there is a moral law demanding obedience that presupposes not only our power of negation but a power to positively obey morality.

This seems implausible. For when we learn as children to deny and defy the commands of our parents, we learn to positively make up our mind and to positively obey or disobey morality. Hence, we should recognize the power of negation or liberty of indifference as the free will that morality presupposes. It is empirical and fits in with our everyday use of the concept of free will.

Keywords Responsibility • Power of negation • Free will • Liberty of indifference • Kant

U. Steinvorth, *A Brief Presentation of Philosophy and Its History*, https://doi.org/10.1007/978-3-031-72533-3_6

Already Plato had marked out judgments, in his critique of the sophists, as not subject to natural necessities if it follows the ideas. His claim is rooted in the Parmenidean belief in the power of reason to distinguish the right from the wrong, truth from falsity. This belief was developed by the Stoics. They took up Aristotle's claim that deliberation rather than voluntariness is the crucial condition for imputable actions (*NE* 3, 1–3) and distinguished, though not always clearly (Görler 2004 [1977]), between *understanding* a thought, *katalepsis*, and *consenting* (and refusing consent) to it, *synkatathesis*. Epictetus identified the faculty of consenting and refusing consent with the *ego* "that not even Zeus himself can overpower" (*Discourses* I 1, 1904: 3). But he didn't recognize this power as free will, as he also believed that Zeus predetermined the course of the world.

Three centuries later Augustine did, defining the power of consenting to a thought as free will (Frede 2011; Steinvorth 2020, Ch. 8). Descartes, Kant, and the logician Gottlob Frege (*Der Gedanke* 1966 [1919]; cp. Bobzien 2021) also took over the Stoic distinction. To see the importance of the Stoic distinction, we should see its parallels to the distinction between *propositional* and *signal* languages (cp. above Chap. 2) drawn by Bühler (1918, 1934) and Popper (1972, Ch. 6, xiv), similar to Chomsky's (1959) distinction of *human languages* from Skinner's (1957) *verbal behavior*.

An example of a signal (not a sign of sign language, which is one of the many species of the propositional language) is the behavior of a bird that "may be ready to fly away, and may express this by exhibiting certain symptoms. These may then release or trigger a certain response or reaction in a second bird, and as a consequence it too may get ready to fly away" (Popper 1972/1979: 235). If the first bird's behavior can occur without triggering the behavior of another bird, it is only a *symptom*; if the behavior of the first and the second bird "always occur together", the first behavior is also a *signal* (236). In contrast, the human language has not only the signaling and the expressive function of signal languages, but also a descriptive and an argumentative function.

To explicate what this means I use terms taken from Frege (1966 [1919]) and the Stoics. It means that only speakers of a propositional language can find in signals a thought (represented in logic by p; for instance, the thought *that there is danger close by)* and can express it both in an imperative (!p, *Danger, flee!*) *and* in an affirmative sentence (⊢-p, *There is danger close by.*). Propositional language enables us to distinguish between a thought, an imperative, its affirmation, its negation, its questioning, and other "speech acts", as Austin (1962) called actions on a thought.

Austin and his student John Searle wanted to show by their speech act theory what we can do with *words*. This is an important aspect of their theory but for philosophy's history it is more important that it shows what we can do with *thoughts*. Using propositional language implies having the concept of truth, while signal languages allow their users only to send and receive news. They cannot distinguish the thought from the speech acts, nor choose whether to say yes or no to a thought they understand. Their behavior is determined in the way animals are determined, while users of a propositional language attain a new level of behavior, as they can stop passing from understanding to obeying the thought. What enables them to do this is their power of judgment. It's not a power of knowing or learning something, but a power to say no as well as yes to what we understand. Because they assume this power, Cartesians, Kantians, and Fregeans find in judgments proof of free will and responsibility.

Kant followed the Stoic view of judging as saying yes or no to a thought when he said about a judging subject:

> It must regard itself as the author of its principles independently of alien influences; consequently it must ... be regarded by itself as free, i.e., the will of a rational being can be a will of its own only under the idea of freedom and must therefore with a practical aim be attributed to all rational beings. (*Groundwork* tr. Wood 2002: 65)

Like the Stoics, Kant distinguishes between understanding a thought and the act of judging it as the decision to say yes or no to it, and like Epictetus, he claims that this decision is necessarily considered free by the judging subject, as it seems to depend only on the subject's choice of a yes or a no to its thought. For Epictetus, my power of negation is enough to prevent Zeus from overpowering me, and so thought Augustine, yet recognizing, more consistently than Epictetus, this power as the power of free will that does make our judgment independent even of God, alarming though this consequence was also for Augustine. Scholastics and Descartes followed suit.

Recognizing judging as an act that proves our ability to act without being necessitated was a momentous philosophical achievement that revolutionized the world no less than establishing science as the judge on the reality question. But no less than for the idea of *free will* that I'll follow in the rest of this chapter was the recognition important for the understanding of *truth*. For truth is something that we are under *pressure to recognize* as true; this is why Protagoras and his modern followers can argue that truth is something we are *necessitated*, by nature or society, to recognize. Insisting that judging is an act of free will implies a distinction between two pressures to recognize something as true, *necessitation* that leaves no space for free will, and *obligation* that does, hence a clarification of a most important obstacle to fully understanding truth.

Kant thought the power of negation that enables us to judge with free will is not enough to make the rational subject independent of alien influences; it decouples us from the chains of causality only if while or after using it we are not again determined by whims or other accidents. The power of negation, which he calls *Freiheit der Willkür, liberty of arbitrariness* or arbitrary liberty (MM ed. Mary Gregor 1991: 52), is for him something we may compare to a random generator that doesn't yet give us autonomy or a will of our own. To become autonomous, "we must necessarily lend to every rational being that has a will also the idea of freedom, under which alone it would act" (2002: 64f). Kant's point is that a *rational* being—a user of a propositional language that can understand a thought without assenting to it—acts autonomously only if it submits to the idea of freedom "under which alone it would act". What Kant understands by this condition is something Scholastics and Descartes to some extent recognize.

For they distinguish between the freedom of indifference, the power to say yes or no to a thought that Kant calls *arbitrary liberty*, and *perfect freedom* that Kant calls autonomy. Yet unlike Kant they understand the freedom of indifference as the freedom of will that makes us responsible, while perfect liberty gives us a will that we may call autonomous, though they don't use this term, but *presupposes* free will. Descartes follows this distinction in his 4th *Meditation*, which can confuse you if you don't note that perfect liberty, though different from the liberty of indifference, *presupposes* free will. But Kant claims our judgment is free only if it presupposes autonomy. Who is right?

Let's listen to Kant. "Die Freiheit der Willkür", he says, translated by Gregor as "freedom of choice", which would be better translated as *arbitrary liberty*, "cannot be defined—as some" (Scholastics and Descartes) "have tried to define it—as the capacity to make a choice for or against the law (*libertas indifferentiae*)". Free will is not the liberty of indifference or what I call the power of negation, because, Kant says, we know freedom (as it first becomes manifest to us through the moral law) only as a *negative* property in us, namely that of not being *necessitated* to act through any sensible determining grounds. But ... although experience shows that man as a *sensible* being has the capacity to choose in opposition to as well as in conformity with the law ... (w)e can also see that freedom can never be located in a rational subject's being able to make a choice in opposition to his (lawgiving) reason, even though experience proves often enough that this happens (though we still cannot conceive how this is possible). (MM 1991: 52; [n.d.] 1900, vol. 6: 226)

Kant, admitting that experience tells us that we have the power to act also against "law", insists that we "never" (*nimmermehr, never ever* is the emphatic German word) must understand the empirically observable arbitrary liberty, the power of negation or the Scholastic liberty of indifference as "freedom" of the will. How can he wipe away the empirical counterevidence? Because he believes that we can gain free will, the capacity that makes us responsible agents rather than trainable cattle, only if we obey reason. I reconstruct his argument thus:

Our liberty of indifference is only the "negative" power of "not being *necessitated*" by "sensible determining grounds", that is, by natural causes, such as desires and interests: let's call them *inclinations*. Yet we know this power, which is the liberty of indifference or the power of negation, only because "it first becomes manifest to us through the moral law", as morality often commands us to act against inclinations. Hence Kant infers that our "negative" empirically observable power of negation is grounded in a positive power that enables us to act against inclinations. This positive power consists in our following "lawgiving reason". Lawgiving reason is rationality applied to our actions, and such rationality is the moral law. Hence, to follow reason means to obey the moral law. For, analyzing morality, Kant finds out that morality commands acting only by maxims that don't imply self-contradiction or self-destruction if everyone acts by them. This command is his *categorical imperative*. So, we attain the *positive* power of liberty, the condition of its negative power, only by obeying the categorical imperative.

Can we agree? The first reason we cannot is that we know to have the "negative" power of "not being *necessitated*" not because we know we can obey the moral law against inclinations. Rather, it is through an entirely morality-indifferent experience that we learn we can act against any kind of rule. Children learn it in their so-called defiant age, the "terrible twos" that to the despair of their parents don't stop when kids become three years old. Tell a kid she should put on a cap because it's cold, and she will throw it off, tell her she should drink her milk slowly, and she will drink it at a gulp. When kids learn our propositional language, they learn they can understand a command as a thought that they can say no to. They discover this power and use it regardless of morality, as it is always fun using one's powers. It's a power of negation, but no negative power that presupposes a "positive" one. They learn not only what to do with the *word* "No", but what to do with a *thought*—to refuse obedience.

There is an even graver reason not to agree with Kant's argument. It implies that we are responsible only for actions that conform to lawgiving reason, that is, only for our moral actions. Immoral actions are not willed by lawgiving reason; they are actions only of a "*sensible*", a *sensual* being, not the actions willed by the self that we become when we obey reason and attain morality, autonomy, and free will at a slap. Kant's free will disables immoral actions. But we assume free will to explain how we can act immorally; Kant turns a *condition* to act both morally and immorally into a *result* of morality. His argument is a paradigm of an *argumentum ad absurdum*, an argument whose conclusion proves that at least one of its premises is false. Kant's false premise is obvious: that we attain free will and responsibility only by what he calls autonomy, obedience to the moral law that is "lawgiving reason". We attain them already with our power of negation, discovering and exercising it in the "terrible twos".

Hence, Kant has no reason to distrust the experience that, as he admits, does tell us that we have in arbitrary liberty a power to act even against lawgiving reason. Hence, he has no reason to define free will as "a pure transcendental idea, which, first, contains nothing borrowed from experience, and second, the object of which also cannot be given determinately in any experience" (B 561, tr. Guyer and Wood). This definition presupposes a supernatural realm to escape naturalistic monism that bans free will from the realm of experience. Scholastics don't object to a supernatural realm but to Kant's exclusion of free will from experience. In our institutions of justice and education, we distinguish between imputable and non-imputable actions and sane and insane individuals. How can we do if free will "cannot be given determinately in any experience"? Hence, we should locate our free will "in a rational subject's being able to make a choice in opposition to his (lawgiving) reason", as the Scholastics and Descartes did, and acknowledge free will as the liberty of indifference or the power of negation.

But we can and should agree with Kant that though the power of negation is free will and makes us responsible, it doesn't give us autonomy. Though free will decouples us from the chains of causality, it doesn't also provide us with a gadget to guarantee that we don't become caught again by a predetermining causal chain. As we may deduce from a cybernetic model of organisms with free will, like them we need not only a random generator but also a gizmo that directs our random actions so that they gain a will of their own. Our power of negation works as a random generator, but it cannot transform the random-generated action possibilities into autonomous actions, actions that we have decided without "alien influences".

This part of Kant's argument against understanding free will as the power of negation does find a confirmation in the Scholastic distinction between liberty of indifference and perfect liberty, which yet doesn't confirm Kant's claim that liberty of indifference is not free will. Descartes, in his 4th Meditation, agrees that for the liberty of indifference to become more than *arbitrary* liberty it must become *perfect*. *Perfect liberty* presupposes the liberty of indifference, hence free will, but to be free, Descartes says, I needn't incline equally to the yes or no of the liberty of indifference; "on the contrary, the more I incline in one direction ... the freer is my choice" (tr. Cottingham 1996: 40). He implies that I become free of what Kant calls "alien influences" only by the perfect liberty that consists in being able to recognize and do what I incline to, yet without losing my liberty of indifference. Kant thinks that I abandon free will if I follow what I incline to, while Descartes thinks I am more perfectly free if I do what I incline to as long as I might also not follow my inclination. He agrees with Kant that liberty of indifference is not enough for what we may call autonomy but finds what is needed in addition not in "lawgiving reason" but simply in sticking to our preferences—which may be piety as well as profit, a life for science as well as a life for sex.

To sum up this chapter, the Stoic tradition finds free will in a power to refuse consent to thoughts, but autonomy or a self of our own in a power to subject our actions to a principle, which Kant says is to be rational, hence moral, and Descartes says is to follow one's inclination without losing free will. By contrast, the Hobbesian tradition considers judgments as predetermined as any other act of an animal. Science has not yet decided which side is right, but we can now see the reasons why (in addition to the argument that people can falsify predictions made about them) the pro-free will party expects science to decide for it.

LITERATURE

Austin, John L. *How to Do Things With Words.* Cambridge/Mass. 1962

Bobzien, Susanne. *Determinism, Freedom, and Moral Responsibility. Essays in Ancient Philosophy.* Oxford: OUP 2021

Bühler, Karl. *Die geistige Entwicklung des Kindes.* Jena: Fischer 1918

Bühler, Karl. Die geistige Entwicklung des Kindes. Jena: Fischer. *Sprachtheorie. Die Darstellungsfunktion der Sprache.* Jena: Fischer 1934

Chomsky, Noam. "A Review of B. F. Skinner's Verbal Behavior". *Language* 35, 1959, pp. 26–58.

Descartes, René. *Meditations on First Philosophy: With Selections from the Objections and Replies,* Cambridge: Cambridge UP, tr. Cottingham, 1996

Epictetus, *Discourses. Tr. George Long.* New York: Appleton 1904

Frede, Michael. Essays in Ancient Philosophy, University of Minnesota Press, Minneapolis. *A Free Will: Origins of the Notion in Ancient Thought.* Ed. A. A. Long. Oakland: Univ. of California Pr. 2011

Frege, Gottlob. "Sinn und Bedeutung". "Der Gedanke" (1919). In *Logische Untersuchungen.* Ed. G. Patzig. Göttingen: Vandenhoeck 1966, 30–53

Görler, Woldemar. "Asthenês synkatathesis: Zur stoischen Erkenntnistheorie". *Würzburger Jahrbücher für die Altertumswissenschaft,* N.F. 3; 1977, 83–92. Reprint in *Kleine Schriften zur hellenistisch-römischen Philosophie;* ed. C. Catrein, Philosophia antiqua 95, Leiden/Boston 2004: 1–15

Kant, Immanuel. n.d. *Gesammelte Werke.* Berlin: Königlich Preußische Akademie der Wissenschaften, Berlin 1900ff

Kant, Immanuel. *Groundwork for the Metaphysics of Morals,* ed. and tr. Allen W. Wood, Yale UP, Wood 2002

Kant, Immanuel. *The Metaphysics of Morals,* tr. Mary Gregor. New York: Cambridge UP 1991

Popper, Karl. *Objective Knowledge.* Oxford: Clarendon 1972,

Skinner, B.F. *Verbal Behavior.* New York: Appleton-Century-Crofts 1957

Steinvorth, Ulrich. "Zur Legitimität des Klonens." In Ludger Schwarte, Hg., Körper und Recht: anthropologische Dimensionen der Rechtsphilosophie. München: Fink. *A Secular Absolute. How Modern Philosophy Discovered Authenticity.* Palgrave Macmillan, New York 2020

CHAPTER 7

Morality, or Schopenhauer

Abstract Modern science dethroned philosophy from answering the reality question; Enlightenment dethroned it from answering the meaning question. For Enlightenment declared the meaning question to exceed the powers of our reason. Morality or the norms of our behavior seemed to be left as the genuine subject of philosophy. Yet what is left of morality if we lack free will that makes us responsible?

We must still take account of the empirical fact that we do recognize principles that people agree are moral. Such is the double imperative, pointed to by Schopenhauer, that we should not harm anyone and help everyone, as far as we can. We can also show that some animals obey similar moral norms. Such demonstrations, though, belong to empirical science. There is still the non-empirical question of why we should go on obeying principles that we seem to have inherited from our animal ancestors. When we look for norms to justify obeying morality, we must distinguish, I argue, between moral and metaphysical norms, or morality and practical metaphysics. For if the grounds for obeying moral norms are again moral norms, we can repeat the question for the reasons to obey *moral* norms.

Unlike moral norms, metaphysical norms refer to ideas of the meaning of the world. Though moral norms can be justified only by metaphysical ones, metaphysical norms cannot override moral ones. Moral norms invalidate metaphysical norms that contradict them because if the latter were

U. Steinvorth, *A Brief Presentation of Philosophy and Its History*,
https://doi.org/10.1007/978-3-031-72533-3_7

valid, following them would end up in destroying the life that morality commands us to protect and that metaphysics and religion want to find a meaning for. Thus, we can understand philosophy's interest in morality as a consequence of its basic meaning question; philosophy's interest proves to be that of setting limits to metaphysical norms.

Keywords Enlightenment • The meaning question • Morality • Practical metaphysics • Religion

Now, what is morality if neither applied rationality nor autonomy, as Kant claimed? This question is important as my claim that all philosophy asks the reality or the meaning question is refuted by the fact that practical philosophy asks which norms are universally valid and why, rather than one of those questions. Yet my claim implies a *persuasive* definition of philosophy. I argue we *can* understand practical philosophy as implicitly asking the meaning question and that, to understand philosophy as fundamental, applying to everything, and to make it great again, we *should understand it as fundamental.* Up to now, I tried to describe philosophy's history; henceforth, I add the perspective of what philosophy should be.

Arthur Schopenhauer provides a concept of morality that props the understanding I argue for, though he isn't likely to accept the use I make of his concept. Philosophers agree, he said, that morality is what is commanded by the double imperative *Neminem laede, imo omnes quantum potes iuva, injure no one, but help all as much as you can* (1977: 76f, §6). Indeed, already Augustine described "the eternal law", as he calls morality, by the imperative "that a man, in the first place, injure no one, and, in the second, do good to every one he can reach" (*CD* 19, 14, tr. Dods).

Thus defining morality, Schopenhauer takes it as a *fact*. To understand it, we have to consider its peculiarities. Like Aristotle, he insists on the priority of the question of *what* things are over the question of *why* they are what they are. So, let's look at morality's peculiarities that Schopenhauer's empiricist approach has us see.

To begin with, there is a terminological implication. Utilitarians claim we should maximize happiness regardless of the double imperative; perhaps they are right, but what they argue for is not morality. When Kant argues that morality is rationality applied to actions, or Nietzsche that traditional morality is the resentment of the weak against the strong and true morality is obedience to the superman, they may propagate recommendable norms, but Schopenhauer implies the norms aren't moral. For the double imperative doesn't demand obedience to rationality or to superman.

Next, the currently prevalent moral theory, contract theory, must be false. Contract theory interprets the prohibition of injury as a result of individuals' right of self-determination, supporting democracy and Protagoras, while by Schopenhauer's approach rights result from the prohibition of injury. If people agree on what later proves bad, the contract theory says it is moral nonetheless, as the contractors bear the consequences of their own decisions. Jonas (1979) pointed to the weakness of this argument, for what people agree on often concerns later generations. As Schopenhauer's approach commits him to describing morality rather than explaining it, he can avoid objections that can probably refute any explanation of morality, also his own explanation of morality by compassion. Yet most remarkable are the peculiarities of morality that Schopenhauer's approach has us see.

First, it forces us to see the importance of the first part of the double imperative, the *prohibition of injury*. Utilitarian and moral theories that in explaining morality give prominence to pity and love of neighbor tend to understand rules of justice, which the first part of the double imperative sums up, as consequences of the rules of help that the second part sums up. This understanding fits in with an evolutionary understanding of morality, as societies favoring norms of mutual help have obvious survival benefits. Thus, it was a surprise when ethologists found that some primates insist on being equally treated, which we can understand as implied by the prohibition of injury. The most ocular evidence is a video by Frans de Waal (2013) showing a capuchin going wild when offered as a reward for some action not tasty grapes that a fellow capuchin is rewarded with but pieces of cucumber, though he accepts the cucumber when his fellow gets it. Perhaps the Capuchin law of equal treatment doesn't increase the Capuchin societies' survival chances, but the Capuchin individuals seem to consider it *their* survival condition. Hence, though this may require revising Darwinist selection principles, we can understand morality as serving mankind's survival, but as serving its survival including the respect of individuals' equality. In any case, the Capuchins show the justice part of the double imperative to have its own help-independent importance.

Second, Schopenhauer's approach has us see the brute force moral norms have on us. Kant pointed to that force when he stressed that moral laws are *categorical* (so that Kant is said to be a moral rigorist), while most other Enlightenment philosophers, explaining morality as norms to promote societies' happiness, presented moral laws as hypothetical only, that is, *valid only if* we pursue happiness. Perhaps Kant called the moral law *categorical* to also indicate that the moral law is as constitutive of the realm of autonomy as his categories of the understanding are constitutive of the realm of nature, but he also called it so for its rigor. Moral norms can have the nearly unescapable grip of taboos, regardless of considerations of happiness. For Enlightenment and utilitarianism, taboos are weird, for Schopenhauer's approach, they are typically moral. Along with its rigor goes, *third*, morality's lack of a cue why we ought to be moral, the question Schopenhauer stated philosophers are quarreling about. Again, it's Kant's merit to insist on the *"incomprehensibility"* of the "practical unconditioned necessity of the moral imperative" (Gr. ed. Wood 79). *Fourth*, we can loosen morality's grasp on us, due to our power of negation.

These four peculiarities explain why there are so many different moral theories, for they show morality as an enigma. But there is a *fifth* peculiarity, most important by its consequences for the question whether moral problems can be understood as answers to the meaning question, that shows morality to be rather shallow than enigmatic. Morality is *not enough to guide our life*. This peculiarity becomes obvious when we look at questions that we may call *existential*. Such are questions as who to live with, which job to choose, or when to have a child. The questions are often morally indifferent. Whether I live with M or N, or am a plumber rather than a doctor, or have a child this year or in three, morally it's often as broad as it is long. But for my existence the difference couldn't be greater.

Morality cannot guide us here, although existentialist philosophers have made existential problems a paradigm of moral problems, to argue that morality is authenticity. But though there are good reasons to claim that a life of authenticity is good and worth pursuing, authenticity is not commanded by morality but by a practical metaphysics, by a view on the meaning of the world that allows deriving norms. To solve existential problems, Enlightenment philosophers and politicians, spiritual directors and psychotherapists advise asking our conscience. They expect our conscience to indicate ideas about the meaning of the world that oblige us, but only as individuals. Such ideas, they thought, cannot oblige societies, as they lack universal validity. Hence, Frederick II, Kant's revered enlightened prince, said, "Everyone should have their own paradise" (in 1740; Lehmann 1881: 4), implying that everyone may follow their own idea of the meaning of the world, but must be moral and abide by the law:

morality is universally valid and the law is rightly enforceable, while ideas about the meaning of the world or life, though needed, are not.

Frederick held the same belief in people's right of having their own ideas of the meaning of the world that the contemporary American Declaration of Independence of 1776 expressed by declaring the pursuit of happiness one of the "unalienable Rights" that today are called human rights. Both adhered to the Enlightenment faith that individuals are the source of any obligation, whether moral or arising from ideas of "paradise", that is, of the meaning of the world or life. They believed the two obligations to arise from the one source of all obligation, the individuals' equal right of self-determination, implying, first, that we need not distinguish between the moral and the metaphysical; second, that the liberty to choose one's religion and meaning of the world is private only and if norms are to be public and universally obliging, then everyone's liberty must be subjected to their mutual compatibility. Hence, right is "the sum of the conditions under which the choice of one can be united with the choice of another in accordance with a universal law of freedom", as Kant said (*Metaph. Of Morals* §B, tr. Gregor).

The Enlightenment distinction between the private and the public might be acceptable if there were existential problems only for individuals, solvable by rules of only private obligation. But there are existential problems also for societies that need universal obligation. Current societies face choices about how to use genetic engineering, artificial intelligence, and other technologies. Many philosophers believe that such questions are moral. But like in individuals' existential problems the options are often morally indifferent. There is no *moral* rule forbidding the cloning of people, as Habermas claimed (1998; cp. Steinvorth 2003, cp. next chapter on ethics committees). When we allow cloning a child we do her as little injustice as when we allow identical twins to be born.

In religious societies, both individual and social existential questions are decided by religions, which means by their ideas of the meaning of the world. For providing a society with meaning is, according to current theorists of religion (Pargament 1997; Pals 2015), the defining task by which to distinguish religions from other basic institutions such as art, science, politics, or the family. Yet Enlightenment philosophers believed that religions' providing societies with meaning can be entirely taken over by morality. They interpreted obligations resulting from religious or metaphysical ideas as *private moral* rather than *metaphysical* norms. But this interpretation is untenable since like individuals, societies face existential problems that are morally indifferent and yet should not be settled by dicing. Secular societies need practical metaphysics as much as religious societies need religion.

Once we acknowledge that besides morality there is the non-moral and yet possibly universal obligation of practical metaphysics, we can understand morality's relation to the meaning question that I claim practical philosophy is implicitly answering. Religion responds to the meaning question in a pre-rational, practical metaphysics in a rational way. Both provide ideas about the meaning of the world. The Enlightenment took such ideas as only privately obliging, yet to solve existential social problems they should be universally obliging. Morality, by contrast, is independent of the meaning question, and for this reason can restrict the norms of religion and of practical metaphysics by its double imperative. Moral norms are only indirect responses to the meaning question via metaphysical norms. Yet we feel them to be more important, as they restrict metaphysical norms.

But why should we restrict metaphysical norms by morality? Why should we give priority to moral over metaphysical norms? The Enlightenment said we should because only moral norms are universal. But if we follow Schopenhauer, then morality is but a fact, and facts, whether natural or moral, cannot oblige us, once we have understood them to be facts, not even privately. By contrast, practical metaphysics presents not facts but meanings that are the very things to oblige us. Hence, moral norms can only restrict metaphysical ones if we find a meaning in them that can override the obligation of metaphysical norms. Such meaning, I think, is that of serving mankind's survival in a way that respects individuals' equality, while the meaning provided by practical metaphysics relates to the ends of the life that morality is to protect. If we thus distinguish between moral and metaphysical norms, then we may well argue that in cases of conflict, moral norms ought to have priority because we first need to protect human life before we can set ends to it, howsoever we may claim universal obligation for them.

The Enlightenment, though, tried to derive all obligation from the sovereign power of individuals rather than from the meaning of "it all". Yet ideologies did so, but without the standards of rationality maintained by philosophy in the tradition of both Enlightenment and Plato. The result was the tragedy announced.

LITERATURE

Habermas, Jürgen. "Genetische Sklavenherrschaft? Moralische Grenzen reproduktionsmedizinischer Fortschritte". *Die postnationale Konstellation*. Frankfurt: Suhrkamp, 1998, pp. 243–247

Jonas, Hans. "Gnosis and Modern Nihilism", Social Research 19. *Das Prinzip Verantwortung—Versuch einer Ethik für die technologische Zivilisation*. Frankfurt: Suhrkamp 1979

Lehmann, Max. *Preußen und die katholische Kirche seit 1640. 2. Theil 1740–1747.* Leipzig: Hirzel, 1881

Pals, Daniel. *Nine Theories of Religion*, New York: Oxford UP 2015

Pargament, Kenneth. *The Psychology of Religion and Coping. Theory, Research, Practice.* New York: Guilford Pr. 1997

Schopenhauer, Arthur. The World as Will and Representation, tr. E.F.G. Payne, New York: Hafner. *Preisschrift über die Grundlage der Moral* (1841), in *Werke in zehn Bänden*, Band VI, Zürich 1977

Steinvorth, Ulrich. "Zur Legitimität des Klonens." In Ludger Schwarte, Hg., *Körper und Recht: anthropologische Dimensionen der Rechtsphilosophie.* München: Fink 2003, 289–302

de Waal, Frans. https://www.youtube.com/watch?v=meiU6TxysCg (2013). Obtained July 30, 2023

CHAPTER 8

Religion and Practical Metaphysics, or Kant, Feynman, and Hitler

Abstract When I understand morality as restricting practical metaphysics, I assume that religion, the first though pre-rational form of practical metaphysics, responds to reality *independently* of morality, by answering the question for meaning. This assumption contradicts the Enlightenment view that considers claims on the meaning of the world a pre-rational form of *morality*. But howsoever we understand religion and practical metaphysics, the Enlightenment and most current philosophy insist that claims on the meaning of the world lack universal validity.

The problem with this claim is that there are existential problems of society, e.g., which technologies to admit to society, that seem to be morally indifferent but nonetheless need solutions that should follow universally valid rules. If morality is indifferent, it should be meaning-oriented practical metaphysics that decides. In fact, even if existential problems are not consciously solved but decided by accident or by the most powerful interests, the result is that society takes on a certain meaning. For instance, if we allow the cloning of human beings, society gets another meaning than if we forbid it (Huxley's *Brave New World,* which allows cloning, has another meaning than a society that forbids it.)

When the Enlightenment banned judgments on the meaning of things from science, the history of philosophy became a catastrophe and a tragedy. In the nineteenth century, the most urgent existential problems of society were how to prevent industrialization from destroying societies.

U. Steinvorth, *A Brief Presentation of Philosophy and Its History,*
https://doi.org/10.1007/978-3-031-72533-3_8

The Enlightenment said they cannot be scientifically solved, as science cannot make claims on the meaning of the world. In contrast, the *ideologists* claimed they could scientifically prove what the goal of history is that does guide us to solve existential social problems. Masses followed them, but they led into the disasters of totalitarian societies.

To stop them, we cannot insist morality must solve the problem (though morality, too, is banned from science, its use is considered justified by the social contract theory or another philosophy), since many existential problems are morally indifferent. Rather, philosophy must show that something rational and universally obliging can be said on the meaning of the world that can tell us how to manage existential social questions.

Keywords Practical metaphysics • Existential problems • The Enlightenment • The tragedy of philosophy • Ideology • Hitler

When theorists ascribe to religion the defining goal of providing a society with meaning, they allow imagining that religions arose from rituals to prepare for and express emotions about important events: a hunt, a war, the birth of a child. To become religious, such rituals must be understood as having a similar point, say, to gain the favor of superhuman powers that people see their life depend on. In some religions, such as Judaism, this favor is understood not as the favor of the divine to help people satisfy their desires but to help find them *more,* which I think we can call *meaning* of life or the world. It needn't be explicit and can result from following the order of daily and yearly prescriptions and recommendations of prayers and thanksgivings, feasts and fasts, processions and pilgrimages. The importance of this meaning-implying order appears in its use to solve problems that are morally indifferent.

In evolution, religion is a later achievement than morality (if morality is a product of evolution). Religions are a specifically human rather than a more general primate survival condition. They offer an order in which humans *find* meaning rather than inventing it. A meaning of the world that we invent cannot serve what we need it for: to make life conditions difficult to accept acceptable. Most important among such conditions are that we haven't been asked if we wanted the life we have been born into and that our life is mortal and short and often gives more pain than pleasure. Like theodicies, the orders that religions offer to find meaning in have us believe that the evil we suffer is an unavoidable part of a whole that is good. But religions demand of their believers unconditional obedience; hence, when people started discussing what is rational to believe, the orders of religions were replaced by the orders of what I call practical metaphysics and of ideologies, which, as we'll see, are a form of practical metaphysics.

Religions and practical metaphysics, and the theodicies that they often imply, provide answers to the meaning question by which, together with the reality question, I want to define philosophy. Hence, they either belong to philosophy or, like religions, are a pre-rational form of philosophy. When the Enlightenment declared human reason to be unable to answer the meaning question, it implied that answers to the meaning question can be true but necessarily lack universal obligation. As Kant said at the very beginning of his *Critique of Pure Reason* (A vii):

> Human reason ... is burdened with questions which it cannot dismiss, since they are given to it as problems by the nature of reason itself, but which it also cannot answer, since they transcend every capacity of human reason.

In fact, Kant does answer the questions, but claims it is not knowledge that his answer provides but faith: "I had to deny knowledge in order to make room for faith" (B xxx). Yet what he says is faith is neither the Christian or another religious faith but belief in the very Cartesian ideas of God, free will, and immortality, that in his *Critique of Pure Reason* he argued are rationally untenable but in his *Preface* to his *Critique of Practical Reason* declared must "be assumed even without our theoretically cognizing and having insight into them" (2002 [1789]: 6).

To stay moral, Kant tells us, we need to *believe* in God, free will, and immortality, though we don't *know* anything about them; hence, the universal obligation of morality cannot result from ideas that find meaning in the world but needs another source. What that source is has been more clearly spoken out by Locke and other contract theorists as well as by the American rebels and Frederick II: it is the sovereign individual who has the basic right of self-determination and can delegate it to a born sovereign or to representatives of the individuals who constitute the society that by its representatives creates laws that oblige "universally", that is, this society.

Enlightenment belief in the sovereignty of the individual supported the English monarchs and Frederick II but became popular by supporting democratic ideas. Yet democracy justifies the rule of majorities even if their rule offends natural law that Locke and Kant expected to be justified as protecting the sovereign individual (Steinvorth 2023, Ch. 23–26). Belief in the sovereign individual split into the political theory that the sovereign individual justifies the rule of majorities and belief in the rule of law or the *Rechtsstaat* that considers democracy only a means to strengthen the rule of law but avoids clearly saying so as it doesn't want to be attacked as anti-democratic.

In contrast to the Enlightenment tradition, ideologists use ideas of the rule of majorities and of the meaning of the world and of history to offer to modern societies metaphysical norms that can solve existential social problems that morality proves unable to solve. Their norms find many adherents because societies face existential problems in need of norms of universal obligation that morality cannot solve. Yet the ideological norms people followed have led them to the disasters of the last centuries. What thus happened to philosophy is the tragedy of philosophy that I announced in Chap. 1. Ideologists were philosophers too. They appealed to the Enlightenment sovereign individual, but to justify their claims on the meaning of the world, they appealed to science. Here, they rehabilitated Protagoras, for they argued that science shows that people are necessitated, by the laws of nature and history, to distinguish between true and false and right and wrong, so that man rather than reality is the measure of truth.

Thus, philosophy split. One party claimed with Kant that the meaning question cannot be rationally answered, the other trusted in human judgment if it is helped by insight in human history and political movements. From a philosophical viewpoint, they split only on the surface of public perception. The initiators of the two most important ideologies, communism and fascism, Marx and Nietzsche, are recognized philosophers today. But for politics, the split was disastrous, as it made philosophy sharpen and deepen the social conflicts that led to the catastrophes of the last centuries, rather than helping solve them by reflection. Both the Enlightenment and the ideologists' errors were venial sins; to use a term of Aristotle's *Poetics*, they were the *hamartiai* that trigger the tragedies.

I'll look at the ideologies in the next chapter. The misery of the part of philosophy that rejects ideology appears in three failures: in its *insecurity about its tasks,* its *blindness to practical metaphysics,* and its *loss of social importance.*

Insecurity about its tasks can be best seen in its funny anecdotical form. When quantum theorist Richard Feynman, to shed light on the obscurities of his subject, asked the question of "the meaning of the world without any living thing on it", "the meaning of life", and "the meaning of it all" (1963/1998), philosophers pricked up their ears. A physicist, a Nobel Prize winner, took up the question they had learned to call pseudo problem and naïve. Wow, then the question cannot be so stupid after all. A quarter of a century later Nagel titled his *Very Short Introduction to Philosophy* with Feynman's question "What Does it all Mean?".

Blindness to practical metaphysics appears in the understanding of committees appointed to think about existential social questions, such as what kinds of technology and of work to admit. Though the options deliberated are often morally indifferent, the committees are called *ethics* committees, following the Enlightenment idea that all obligation springs from individuals' right of self-determination. This idea eclipses the need to look for what the next generations rather than we want their life or the world to be and to mean, hence, for an acceptable practical metaphysics.

Loss of social importance becomes embarrassing when we look at how little recognized philosophy did to stop ideologies from influencing people. Here is an example of ideology that wasn't stopped by philosophy:

> Man must never succumb to the lunacy (*Irrsinn*) to believe he has really risen to being lord and master of nature ... he must grasp the fundamental necessity of nature's ruling and understand how much also his existence is subjected to the laws of the eternal fight and struggle to the top. Then he will feel that in a world in which planets and suns are circling ... in which strength is the master of weakness, coercing it to obey or breaking it, there is no place for special laws for man. He too is ruled by the eternal principles of this ultimate wisdom. He can try to understand them, but he can never free himself from them. (Hitler 1943 [1925]: 267, my tr.)

Philosophers look down with disgust upon fascist uses of the ideology of social Darwinism but ignore how much they agree with some of its elements. They wouldn't call the view that there is "place for special laws for man" *Irrsinn*, but many agree there is no such place. Nor would they draw the conclusions that Hitler drew. But not to draw them, they need arguments about what can be said on the meaning of the world. Philosophy believed the right way to fight ideology is morality. Yet ideology lives on answers to the same meaning question that once also philosophers wanted to answer. Philosophy must fight ideology on their common battle ground, which is practical metaphysics. Fascism and its success were not an accident, because one cause was the Enlightenment's revocation—or betrayal—of philosophy's original goal to answer the meaning question better than religions did.

Yet the Enlightenment was right to insist on the difficulty answering the meaning question. Kant, Frederick II, and the Declaration of Independence were right to suppose that men's ideas on the meaning of the world are as diverse as religions, that philosophy cannot expect to find a basic principle for the meaning of the world as it can expect to find some for morality, and that therefore everyone should have their own paradise and an eternal right to pursue what they privately believe to be their happiness, provided this belief doesn't offend morality. Yet the Enlightenment erred in concluding that philosophy cannot say anything rational about the meaning of the world. Enlightenment had no doubt about one *acceptance condition* for ideas on the meaning of the world: they must conform to morality. Everyone should have their own paradise—but moral they must be.

Today, too, the so-called ethics committees that are to deliberate existential questions of societies also require that norms to plan the future must conform to logic and science. Yet these acceptance conditions will not be enough to reduce the possible norms of practical metaphysic to a number small enough to guide the future. There is, I claim, a further acceptance condition, controversial though it is: metaphysical ideas must be *progressive*. Before I defend this claim, we should understand why ideologies claim scientificity and superiority to traditional philosophy.

LITERATURE

Feynman, Richard. *The Meaning of it All. Thoughts of a Citizen-Scientist,* Boston: Addison-Wesley 1998 (including lectures held in 1963)

Hitler, Adolf. Mein Kampf. 2 Bde. München: Franz Eher 1925 and 1927. Quoted from the ed. of 1943

Kant, Immanuel. *Critique of Practical Reason* (1789). Tr. Pluhar. Indianapolis/Cambridge: Hackett 2002

Steinvorth, Ulrich. "Zur Legitimität des Klonens." In Ludger Schwarte, Hg., Körper und Recht: anthropologische Dimensionen der Rechtsphilosophie. München: Fink. *Unterdrückung durch Beglückung. Eine liberale Revision der politischen Philosophie.* Hamburg: Meiner 2023

CHAPTER 9

Ideology, or Destutt de Tracy and Marx

Abstract Ideology was founded by the French aristocrat Destutt de Tracy as a science that was to show how impressions impinging on the minds of happiness-seeking intelligent animals develop into systems of ideas that formerly became religions telling us what the meaning of life is and what we should do to conform to it. But today, Tracy argues, scientists can show, by taking account of social conditions, that all religious systems are mistaken and that the best way to happiness is by instituting social division of labor, so everyone can use their talents, and arrange free markets for the exchange made necessary by the division of labor.

Tracy, Marx, and Engels, although the two latter hoped for an exchange without equivalents, understood their ideologies as the most advanced forms of social science. But many philosophers argue that norms, whether moral or metaphysical, cannot be deduced from social facts, as the ideologists implied. Therefore, they cannot provide the metaphysical norms that seem to be necessary to solve existential problems, for such norms lack universal validity.

I propose a solution to this problem. Though we cannot prove positive claims on the meaning of the world, we can find rational *acceptance conditions* for answers to the meaning question. Critics of ideology agree that such answers must conform to the norms of logic, science, and morality. Adding the condition that they conform to what science recognizes as

U. Steinvorth, *A Brief Presentation of Philosophy and Its History*,
https://doi.org/10.1007/978-3-031-72533-3_9

progressive would considerably reduce the number of acceptable candidates for metaphysical answers and norms.

Keywords Ideology • Norms and values • Exchange by and without equivalents • Rational acceptance conditions for metaphysical norms • Progress

Ideologists and their precursors, the sophists, differ from what we may call "recognized" philosophers by thinking judgments are determined by natural and social causes rather than the special free-willed actions that I explained in Chap. 6. But many current philosophers also consider judgments determined by natural and social causes. The difference is today seen in ideologists' trust in political movements that they believe warrant the truth of judgments. So do the two most influential ideologies, communism and fascism, trusting in left-wing and right-wing political movements. But there is also an ideology of liberalism, to be distinguished from a non-ideological liberal political philosophy that defends principles of toleration and power checks. Remarkably, the theorist who introduced the term and the project of an ideology, Destutt de Tracy (1754–1836), was an ideologist of liberalism.

Tracy assumed, like all ideologists, that there is no place for special laws for man; all mental activities, or *passivities*, as they should be better called, are forms of sensations, including judgments (Head 1985: 67–74). He believed we are caused to develop ideas including those of truth and rightness and of a meaning of the world that we should live for. Formerly such ideas formed the systems we know as religions; they organized people's actions to become happy or attain the goal that they considered the meaning of life and included theodicies. At his time, such systems are determined to become a "science of the formation of ideas" that can "replace theology as the dominant unifying system." For today, intellectuals can weed out the errors and superstitions that caused religions and theodicies so that we can "exclude all religious studies whatsoever from the ideological system" (Terrell 1817/1970: i).

Like Locke, Tracy considered the human mind at birth an empty page yet developing not only by the impingements of sense data but also by its desire for happiness. Such a system becomes the science that Tracy called ideology only if it develops without false ideas, say, that some people are witches or that the laws of nature can change. A *science* of the ideas that organize our actions is caused when theorists—"ideologists"—construe a system without false ideas. Such science proves to be liberal, as the ideologist, using science, proves that we best become happy in a market society in which we exchange the fruits of the activities that we are best at. Tracy's ideology lives on in neoliberal theories considered scientific rather than ideological. Yet the word *ideology* lost its tie not to science but to economic liberalism when Marx and Engels criticized the liberalism of their time. But note how they did:

> Just as ... at an earlier period [at the English bourgeois revolution, U. St.], a section of the nobility went over to the bourgeoisie, so now a portion of the bourgeoisie goes over to the proletariat, and in particular, a portion of the bourgeois ideologists, who have raised themselves to the level of comprehending theoretically the historical movement as a whole. (*Communist Manifesto* 1848/2010: 19f)

Marx and Engels, calling themselves bourgeois ideologists, thought it is by *comprehending* history that they were caused to describe the unifying system of ideas that directs our actions, as formerly religions did. Tracy too thought that he was caused to describe his science of ideology by *comprehending* ideas (cp. e.g., 1817/1970: xviii), and so did Nietzsche. As they all believed that the future is determined and that they understood how it was determined, they considered their belief superior to former philosophy that didn't understand future's determination.

But their belief that we must *understand* history kept an element of the idea that judging is special. It implies that because of their education, bourgeois can be better at comprehending than proletarians, or Jews can be better than Aryans. Later ideologists smelled both the Platonist heritage and the claim of the better educated to leadership and justified their claims by appeal to being one of the class, race, or religion, chosen by history, natural selection, or God, to know what mankind is to do, even if they had not studied anything. Yet that they *are* chosen is confirmed only if they gain power. So, it's in seizing power that the second class of ideologists believe.

There is a third class of ideologists. Like the first class, the second takes the difference between true and false and right and wrong seriously, even though their truth criterion is what conduces to their power. The third class consider themselves superior not because they know the truth but because they can make people believe in them without their referring to truth, theory, or understanding. Such a class can arise only when individuals control or dominate the media. Perhaps social influencers and media controllers who want to control societies should not be called ideologists. But they agree with the ideologists of the second class that political questions should be decided by power, not necessarily the power of weapons but by the power of votes, whether rational or not.

Isn't it anyway unimportant how a judgment or theory has arisen, whether causally or rationally, and whether it is true or false? Don't we accept a theory if it helps us cope with our environment, for instance, if a prediction based on it is confirmed? We do, but to decide whether it is confirmed, we must judge whether the prediction has come true, hence, must presuppose the importance of a difference between true or false.

Yet ideology is a challenge for philosophy because it satisfies the need for finding an order that indicates what has value and where we should go. I call it a tragedy that the Enlightenment revoked philosophy's original claim to answer the meaning question, but it was right that there aren't sufficient reasons for positively stating what the meaning of life is. Yet I claim philosophy can tell us something about metaphysical norms needed in ethics committees and other institutions that are to plan future societies, as it can rationally argue for *acceptance conditions* of practical metaphysical norms. The conditions of conforming to logic, morality, and science, I think, are uncontroversial, but I added the controversial condition of progressiveness. Can this be defended without resort to ideology?

There are historical developments that we can hardly deny being progress. The paradigm is science. It succeeded in predictions and technological applications that changed the world. Technology, in its many forms from agriculture and other branches of production to medicine and weather forecast, is another case of uncontroversial progress.

Besides, think of biological evolution. Isn't its development from the simplest to the most complex forms of life progress? It doesn't show what a creator god intended or meant, but this doesn't imply that there is no progress, regardless of a divine mind. Progress in science and technology can be measured because we presuppose goals, providing better predictions and more effective productions, by which to measure their progress. In contrast, for evolution, we can't indicate such goals, and yet Ernst Mayr was right to claim "that overall there is an advance" in evolution. But we need to distinguish. There is, in science, *technical progress*, measurable by an approach to a recognized goal, and, in evolution, *value progress*, lacking such a goal, but felt as an increase in value.

If progressivity is another acceptance condition for metaphysical norms, and answers to the meaning question, it's value progress that metaphysical norms must conform to. For the acceptance conditions are to also exclude ideologies that imply a goal by which to measure progress, such as the rule of a race or a classless society. Yet may we talk of value progress in science? As the concept of progress is infected by ideological claims on the goals of history, conscientious writers shun it. Moreover, Max Weber, one of the founders of sociology, banned value judgment from social science; hence, it seems also the concept of value progress, as its use implies value judgment.

But Weber also claimed there is a way for sociology to state value progress in history, in contrast to what interpreters, quite naturally, have expected (e.g., Iggers 1965: 8; Torpey 2019). In fact, as I want to show now, he provides an empirically definable concept of value progress that allows philosophy to use conformity to progress as an acceptance condition and to take up its task of answering the meaning question. Hence, though I present philosophy, I look at a sociologist to argue for a philosophy that realizes its potential.

LITERATURE

Destutt de Tracy, Antoine Louis Claude. *A Treatise on Political Economy or Elements of Ideology*, ed. by Thomas Jefferson 1817, reprint New York: Kelley 1970

Head, Brian. *Ideology and Social Science: Destutt de Tracy and French Liberalism.* Dordrecht: M. Nijhoff 1985

Iggers, Georg. "The Idea of Progress: A Critical Reassessment", *The American Historical Review* 71, 1965, pp. 1–17

Marx, Karl, and Friedrich Engels. *The Communist Manifesto.* 1848/2010. https://www.marxists.org/archive/marx/works/download/pdf/Manifesto.pdf. Obtained Oct. 11, 2023

Terrell, Timothy D. *Introduction* to Destutt de Tracy 1817

Torpey, John. "Max Weber and the Idea of Progress". *Max Weber Studies* 19, 2019, pp. 88–105

CHAPTER 10

Progress, or Weber

Abstract Max Weber, one of the founders of sociology, is known for his ban on evaluation from the social sciences. I argue that despite or even because of his ban, Weber finds a way for sociology to evaluate the development of civilizations. He does so by investigating technical progress, which must be purely descriptive, and by using the fact that technical progress can be "entangled" with progress in a normative sense, or with increased value, to state that there is progress in a normative sense. As I understand Weber, although he doesn't say so himself, technical progress entangles increase of value if it is pursued by actions loved for their own sake. For Weber assumes, as I think most people do, that if we do something for its own sake or *autotelically*, then there is value in the action.

Thus, Weber provides an acceptance condition for claims on the meaning of the world: that it requires technical progress in value spheres that must be produced by autotelic actions. Yet it seems he must use two criteria to evaluate societies: how many value spheres there are in a society, and how much autonomy a value sphere has in pursuing its values.

Keywords Banning evaluation from science • Technical progress • Progress in a normative sense • Entanglement • Value spheres • Autotelic action

© The Author(s), under exclusive license to Springer Nature
Switzerland AG 2024
U. Steinvorth, *A Brief Presentation of Philosophy and Its History*,
https://doi.org/10.1007/978-3-031-72533-3_10

In his essay on the *Ethical Neutrality (Wertfreiheit) in Sociology and Economics* Weber states that there is an "absolutely non-evaluative way" to talk of progress "if one identifies it with the 'continuation' of some concrete process of change" (tr. Shils and Finch 1949: 27); for example, the change in treating disease that can be magic or scientific (34f). "But in most cases, the situation is substantially (*wesentlich*) more complicated" (27; Shils and Finch drop the word *wesentlich* in their translation) because there is an "entanglement" of the "absolutely non-evaluative way" to talk of progress "with value-judgments" that "is most intricate" (27). As Weber explains referring to music:

> From the standpoint of the interests of the modern European ... its [music history's] central problem is: why did the development of harmonic music from the universally popularly developed folk polyphony take place only in Europe and in a particular epoch [the Renaissance], whereas everywhere else the rationalization of music took another and most often quite opposite direction: interval development by division (largely the fourth) instead of through the harmonic phrase (the fifth). Thus at the center stands the problem of the origin of the third in its harmonic meaningful interpretation, i.e., as a unit in the triad ... (tr. Shils/Finch 30f)

By describing the change of the *technical* means that allowed for an increase of "artistic expression" and "meaningful interpretation" (Shils 31), the social scientist describes a "quantitative increase" or a "rationalization"; Weber uses this term to describe all kinds of technical progress (e.g., *Prefatory Remark* ed. Kalberg 160). Though describing it "without reference to any evaluations" (Shils 27), the scientist refers to "what is usually bound up with it", a "qualitative diversification of the possible modes of response", which is a *value progress*. This nexus of the quantitative with the qualitative, the technical with value progress gets lost in Shils' and Finch's translation.

For Weber distinguishes between "three meanings of the term 'progress'; (1) merely 'progressive' differentiation [Weber's example is magic], (2) progress of technical rationality in the utilization of means [his example is science], and, finally (3) increase in value" (Shils 34). He says the "Verquickung", *entanglement*, of progress in these three meanings is "repeated", referring to the *Verquickung* mentioned some pages before, aptly translated as "entanglement" (Shils 27). But Shils and Finch now translate *Verquickung* by "widespread confusion", not again by "entanglement", though Weber by speaking of "repeated" *Verquickung* makes clear he means the same as before. They present Weber as claiming that value progress is confounded rather than entangled or "usually bound up with" technical progress.

Yet entanglement of technical with value progress is basic for Weber's concept of progress. This becomes obvious when he reopens the topic of progress in his *Prefatory Remarks* to his *Collected Essays in the Sociology of Religion*. Asking "What combination of circumstances called forth *Kulturerscheinungen* [*cultural phenomena*] that ... arose ... only in the West...?" (Weber 1978 [1920]; Kalberg 149, my tr.), he again relies on the nexus of technical and value progress. The phenomena he describes are in part the same as those explained in *Wertfreiheit* (cp. the music and architecture examples, ed. Shils 29–32, ed. Kalberg 150f), but now he refers to *value spheres* as the place of entanglement; though he doesn't use the term, value spheres are recognizable as the spheres of science, art, politics, and economy. In his *Zwischenbetrachtung (Interim Reflection)* at the end of the same volume, value spheres become his explicit object. He discusses, as historically influential spheres, not as a complete list of value spheres, value spheres that were known from Hegel: family, economy, state, art, religion, and science, plus the sphere of eroticism, which shows how Weber differs from Hegel (cp. Steinvorth 2023: 140). Now, it becomes clear what it is in the process entangled by the technical progress that makes it a *value* progress: that it realizes the value pursued by a value sphere.

For Weber, value spheres are the key to understanding societies, just as the division of labor was for Emile Durkheim (1893), besides Weber the recognized founder of sociology. If the division is primitive, individuals are bound by *mechanical solidarity*, by personal relations that individuals can attain by individual effort. Modern societies need *organic solidarity*, ties that no individual can establish alone. To keep up modern societies, people must understand what is called *Durkheim's paradox*. People strive for *autonomy* or (synonymously used) *individuality*, as the division of labor can require an expertise that experts use for autonomous judgments. As such autonomy is attractive, it becomes a social ideal. But it is based on a division of labor that makes everyone dependent on society. Insisting on autonomy threatens social cohesion, hence survival. Modern society's ideal is suicidal if used without reflection.

Weber, too, regarded the division of labor as basic for societies, but found it accompanied by a formation of value spheres. In their beginning, people lived in the "cycle of the old simple organic rural existence" (Zw 560, cp. 558, my tr.). The division of labor fans out labor, offering different jobs, but also different *autotelic* actions, actions done *for their own sake* in which people discover a value that organizes their life and tells them what they live for. As Weber calls them *value* spheres for this quality, we must understand that to pursue a value necessarily means, for Weber, to pursue it *autotelically,* as an *end in itself.* Yet he implies two criteria to define a value sphere. A value sphere (1) pursues the same value not reducible to another value nor pursued by another sphere or (2) replaces the "old simple organic rural existence"; therefore, value spheres are "life orders", *Lebensordnungen* (Gerth 323, Zw 537).

Criterion (1) defines science, art, religion, the economy, and eroticism; they pursue *only one* value considered irreducible and not pursued by another sphere. Its irreducibility shows in the fact that though a value sphere covers most various branches, think of the various branches of science and art, their agents agree that they use the same standard to rank activities of the same sphere, though modified for the different kinds of a sphere. Criterion (2) defines the family and the state that pursue *different* irreducible values; the family pursues what we may consider the values of procreation, intimacy, and eroticism; the state, the values of managing public affairs, such as waging war or improving a territory's infrastructure, and of enforcing justice. Locke claimed that enforcing justice is the only task of states (*Tr.* II § 124), but he subsumed waging a war and improving the infrastructure under justice enforcement. Yet justice enforcement is measured by its justice and managing public affairs, by its efficiency, and these goals can conflict, so they should be kept apart. As Weber lists both the family and eroticism as value spheres, he uses both (1) and (2) to define value spheres. But only by (1) could he add eroticism to Hegel's spheres and thus indicate the specificity of his concept of a value sphere. So, criterion (1) was more important to Weber.

Using criterion (2) led him to a remarkable difficulty defining the state. States need one goal to judge the priority of their various goals; in fact, this goal became power, as power is the means to get any goal. Thus, Weber ascribed to the state the goal of "successfully claiming the monopoly of legitimate physical coercion", which secures power (*WuG* 1980: 29, my tr., cp. 2019: 136). This conforms to historical facts but deprives the state of the property that makes the pursuit of a goal in a value sphere a *value progress:* that it is done for its own sake. Power, though it turns easily into a goal itself, by its nature is a means for an end in itself, hence, its pursuit cannot be autotelic.

Yet howsoever Weber defined the state, we can point out the *marks of Weber's concept of progress.* We have seen that (1) he claims there is value progress scientifically describable despite the evaluation it implies because it is entangled by technical progress; now we see (2) the sites of such entanglement are the *value spheres,* and we are to see (3) *they entangle value progress* if their pursuit of a goal is done *for its own sake.* For a value sphere is a class of activities pursuing the same irreducible value that can be non-evaluatively described as its *goal.* Thus, the goal of science can be found in explaining nature by falsifiable laws, of politics in efficiently managing public affairs, of economy in sustainably using resources, of religion in providing a meaningful order. In art and eroticism, the goals are controversial, but artists and Don Giovannis agree that there is a specific goal of their activities, difficult though it is to describe. The degree to which the goals are attained can also be non-evaluatively described. But the goals are felt to be values as far as a devotee pursues them *autotelically* rather than as a means for another goal or *heterotelically.* Hence, if a sphere activity is autotelic, technical progress entangles value progress.

As Weber finds in value spheres such an entanglement, he can answer the question for the "combination of circumstances" that "called forth *Kulturerscheinungen*" that distinguish the West. At Weber's time, they were an object of pride of Westerners, expressed by Rudyard Kipling, one year Weber's junior, in his often-quoted poem on "the White Man's burden" ("Take up the White Man's burden—The savage wars of peace—Fill full the mouth of Famine And bid the sickness cease; And when your goal is nearest The end for others sought, Watch Sloth and heathen Folly Bring all your hope to nought", 1899). Weber shared this pride but explained the West's *Sonderweg* by the non-evaluatively describable autonomy, the right to pursue its goals, that the West granted value spheres more than any other civilization did. But he also assumes a reason for the value judgment implied by the pride taken in the West, that the sphere activities are not only technical but also value progress, as far as they are not pursued for power's or money's sake, but autotelically.

Thus, he confirms the pride in the Western civilization but does so only conditionally. For we can infer from his remarks on capitalism in his *Prefatory Remarks* and from his description of twentieth-century capitalism at the end of his *Protestant Ethics* as "an iron cage" (1930: 123) that though he understood modern societies as unions of value spheres, he saw them at his time as dominated by the economic sphere. For capitalism, he says, now controls societies. Hence, he can no longer assign to the technical progress that capitalism stimulated in production and science a value progress entangled in it, as activities are not done autotelically, for their own sake, but heterotelically to raise profits. He implies that Westerners can no longer be proud of what once has been a proud civilization.

There are some notable consequences of Weber's concept of progress. The *first* one pertains to sociology. Sociology is to describe where and how technical progress entangles value progress. Saying something about value progress, sociology implies metaphysical views about values that are not moral; they even show that "ethics is not the only thing in the world that is 'valid'" (*Wertfreiheit*, tr. Shils/Finch 15). Sociology is not metaphysically neutral.

Second, Weber regards the values of the value spheres not as inventions, but as objective and discoverable. The *institutions* of the economic sphere, markets, money, stocks, are inventions but must fit the objective requirements of their sphere value, which is, I assume, the value of a saving use of productive resources. The *institutions* of the political sphere, *poleis,* empires, states, function only if they fit the objective value of effectively managing the public affairs of societies, allowing the political inference that today, nation states have become obsolete, as public affairs require global institutions (Steinvorth 2023). And *truth* is a goal to be *discovered* rather than made by man, and it's a value, as it can be pursued for its own sake, in science and in detective novels. This contradicts ideologies.

Third, Weber's concept of progress bears on traditional liberalism. Kant argued that if we don't make rationality the condition of our arbitrary liberty, which is the power of negation, we'll stay under the alien influence of whims or other causes, while Descartes said that to gain perfect liberty, we should follow our inclinations without losing our power of negation. Weber implies we gain autonomy if we pursue an irreducible value of a value sphere for its own sake. Hence, the first task of liberal law should be to protect value spheres rather than individuals.

The protection of individuals was considered the task of law because individuals were seen as the sources of all obligation, moral or metaphysical (cp. above Chap. 7). Weber rejects this keystone of the Enlightenment, leaving to liberalism the right of individuals to choose their own value sphere and the command to tolerate everyone's choice of their sphere value. By Weber's concept of progress, law is the sum of conditions under which the autonomy of value spheres rather than the liberty of individuals is compatible. This consequence provokes many objections.

For instance, Weber is committed to solving conflicts between entrepreneurs and employees by having the conflict judged by the goal of the sphere of economy, the most economical use of possible productive resources, human resources included. But it is more likely that employees want to solve the conflict by how content a solution will make them, rather than how far a solution will promote the most economical use of productive resources.

The objection can be countered only by conceding that Weber's reformed liberalism presupposes a structuring of societies so that everyone can choose the value sphere they want to dedicate their life to. Such structuring requires a high degree of automation in production so that a small number of people is enough to do the labor necessary in the economic sphere. In a conflict between entrepreneurs and employees, this small number would likely be ready to have the goal of the economic sphere solve the conflict, as they would have chosen the sphere because they love the economical use of resources.

This defense of Weber's liberalism looks utopian but can rely on the current fast increase of automation in production, making increasingly many people economically superfluous and free for autotelic activities in the value sphere of their choice. Much can again be objected, but I could here only sketch a possible defense of Weber.

However, Weber's concept of progress seemed to him to condemn progressive societies to ungovernability and decay. Progressive societies are based on autonomous value spheres. But value spheres "stand in irreconcilable conflict with each other" like the gods of polytheism that he compares them with (*Science as a Vocation*, ed. Gerth 147). They exclude each other; so, even more than organic solidarity, they threaten to tear society up. Still, I think his utopia can be defended. For he didn't duly factor in that there is an irreducible value of justly solving social conflicts, which can develop into an autonomous value sphere if the political sphere is shrunk to that of managing public affairs. In societies that take rights more seriously than democracy, this sphere of justice enforcement has attained relative autonomy and might become a conscious promoter of progress understood as Weber did.

To sum up my description of Weber's concept of progress, it implies a multiple conceptual revolution. It binds value progress to the rise of value spheres, has sociology tell us something about practical metaphysics, contradicts ideology, and replaces the law based on the liberty of individuals by a law protecting the autonomy of value spheres. But most important for our understanding of progress is that Weber conceives progress as splitting into the many value spheres each of which pursues one irreducible value. So strictly speaking there is progress only in a value sphere. If we want to talk of progress in societies, we have to take into account how many of the possible irreducible values have become value spheres, and how far value spheres have attained autonomy, the right to pursue, within the bounds of justice, their values without regard to other values.

There are two problems my description of Weber's concept of progress faces. First, Weber is explicit about technical progress entangling value progress, but what I consider its consequences are my interpretation. Why didn't he state them himself? Perhaps he died too early; perhaps he shrank back from inferring them because this would show that his sociology implies a plea for restructuring society, shaking his ideal of a value-free sociology. Second, why follow it? Because, I claim, progress is a normative but non-moral concept that today is crucial when we look for universally obliging norms that can guide current societies and individuals when morality proves insufficient, and Weber's concept suits most people's ideas of what is good with progress. Hence, even if my Weber interpretation is wrong, the concept I ascribe to him provides a restrictive acceptance condition for metaphysical norms needed to plan the future and to rehabilitate philosophy's task of answering the meaning question.

LITERATURE

Durkheim, Emile. *De la division du travail social.* Paris: Alcan, 1893
Kipling, Rudyard. "The White Man's Burden". *London Times,* 4.2.1899, *New York Tribune* und *The Sun* 5.2. 1899
Steinvorth, Ulrich. "Zur Legitimität des Klonens." In Ludger Schwarte, Hg., Körper und Recht: anthropologische Dimensionen der Rechtsphilosophie. München: Fink. *Unterdrückung durch Beglückung. Eine liberale Revision der politischen Philosophie.* Hamburg: Meiner 2023
Weber, Max. The Protestant Ethic and the Spirit of Capitalism. (1905). Translated by Parsons in 1930. Reedited by Routledge, London 2001; https://selforganizedseminar.wordpress.com/wpcontent/uploads/2011/07/weber_protestant_ethic.pdf
Weber, Max. Economic Ethics of World Religions (1920), ed. G. Roth and C. Wittich: University of California Pr 1978

Weber, Max. Wirtschaft und Gesellschaft (1922). Tübingen: Mohr 1980 (abbr. WG)

Weber, Max. Economy and Society, ed. and tr. Keith Tribe, Cambridge/MA: Harvard UP 2019 (abbr. ES)

Weber, Max. Max Weber on the Methodology of the Social Sciences, tr. and ed. Edward A. Shils and Henry A. Finch. Glencoe/Ill.: Free Press 1949

CHAPTER 11

Applying Weber to Ideologies

Abstract To be progressive, Weber requires society to allow for the autotelic pursuit of the goals of a value sphere. Isn't Weber developing himself
an ideology rather than abolishing them?

We may say so indeed. But he also provides a rational acceptance condition in addition to the conditions of agreeing with our logic, knowledge,
and morality—that claims on the meaning of the world must make sure
that people can act autotelically in a value sphere. This condition implies
that ideologies must not be totalitarian, as autotelic actions in value spheres
are done for their own sake and rule out totalitarianism, which requires
people to act for the values proclaimed by the state.

Keywords Autotelic action • Value spheres • Ideology • Rational
acceptance conditions for metaphysical norms • Totalitarianism

I resorted to Weber to reduce candidates for an acceptable practical metaphysics by requiring them to conform to what science can recognize as
value progress. Weber provides a concept of progress that implies a concept of truth that suits better the Stoic than the ideological view of judgment. But this is not enough to disqualify ideologies as acceptable practical
metaphysics. For the scientist who thinks she *discovers* truth as a property
of a judgment made by free will might be *necessitated* to do so. So, we

should check whether what is essential for ideologies conforms to what Weber requires of value progress. Essential for ideologies, I suppose, is that they make a claim about an order O that tells us what has value and provides meaning and solves existential problems. Any practical metaphysics, religion, and theodicy raise such a claim, so we'll have to judge what makes the O of ideologies unacceptable.

Let us distinguish as the most influential ideologies:

social Darwinism, claiming O is all creatures' "eternal fight and struggle to the top",

Marxism, claiming O is men's fight for satisfying their needs, which is today the fight for a classless society,

fundamentalism, claiming O is being loyal to the God of one's religion or to another transcendent principle, and

liberalism, claiming O is to live the way one likes most.

These ideologies are variations of the "science of the formation of ideas" that Tracy hoped would replace religions "as the dominant unifying system" to shape our responses and help us, as the scientifically confirmed best way, attain happiness or conform to what we consider the meaning of the world. The orders O that I assign to the four ideologies can be variously described and are variously logically related to each other. Marxism can be understood as a variant of liberalism, as the satisfaction of one's needs can be understood as a variant of the life one likes most, and both Marxism and liberalism can be seen as a variant of social Darwinism, and social Darwinism can be seen as a fundamentalism that takes non-human nature as its god. I assume that the four listed ideologies conform to logic, science, and morality. There are versions of them that do not conform to them, but to test them by Weber's concept of progress let's assume they do. Fundamentalism, too, can be formulated to agree with science and morality, for example, by interpreting the order of nature as one's god. How then do ideologies fail Weber's concept?

They fail it if their O requires their adherents to believe in them as unconditionally as religions demand faith of their believers. In contrast, though Weber's O requires its followers to submit to an order that splits societies into value spheres, it allows them to have their own will in choosing their value sphere, which by Weber's standards of value progress should even exist for any possible irreducible value, and therefore isn't what is ordinarily called *totalitarian*. Philosophers can distinguish ideology from non-ideological philosophy by their *truth concept*: ideology follows Protagoras' *homo mensura* thesis or its variation that truth is what man is necessitated, by natural and social laws, to believe to be true; philosophy follows the Platonic and Stoic tradition that truth is what man, by his ability of judging without being necessitated, discovers to be true. Weber's concept of progress sides, as we have seen, with the Platonic tradition, hence by this criterion can be classified as a philosophy rather than an ideology. But the socially important difference between Weber's practical metaphysics and those of the listed ideologies is that the latter are totalitarian and the former isn't. Consequently, if *O* is not totalitarian, as may be the case with versions of liberalism, but also of Marxism and fundamentalism, they do not necessarily fail Weber's concept of progress.

Hence, what disqualifies a practical metaphysics and an answer to the meaning question is not whether it is *ideological*; any answer can be considered ideological, but whether it is *totalitarian* or has totalitarian implications. I'll not try to define totalitarianism (but refer to Aron 1968: 193ff as a helpful discussion); rather, I ask why we should take totalitarianism as disqualifying. One answer is that totalitarianism requires actions to be done for the *O* that a totalitarian ideology maintains, while according to Weber, there is value progress only if actions are done for their own sake rather than for some *O*. Another equally important answer is to point to the attractions of a non-totalitarian *O*. One of them is that it allows everyone to argue about the right *O* and to ask and answer the meaning question, another one is that it allows everyone their own choice of what to do for its own sake and to find value and meaning in.

As Weber finds value progress in autotelic actions entangled in technical progress, we can, if we allow for metaphors, judge what Elon Musk calls the "really big milestones" as advances in value progress: "single-celled life, multicellular life, differentiation of plants and animals, life extending from the oceans to land, mammals, consciousness". For these advances are entangled in the mere "'continuation' of some concrete process of change" (Weber, tr. Shils and Finch 1949: 27) that natural evolution is, and they don't serve a heterotelic goal. We can even follow Musk's conclusion: "On that scale, the next important step is obvious: making life multiplanetary" (Isaacson 2023: 94). Yet we can also state when Musk's or a similar program becomes unacceptable: if its goal becomes a universal obligation and prevents autotelic actions. We *can* though need not understand Musk's concept of progress like Weber's concept as requiring progressive actions to be entangled by technical advances and to be done autotelically.

Musk's making life multiplanetary is, of course, only one of many other projects that meet strict acceptance conditions for answering the meaning question, but it's worth mentioning as it shows that such conditions can justify not only generally accepted projects.

LITERATURE

Aron, Raymond. *Democracy and totalitarianism* (French orig. 1965). London: Weidenfeld and Nicolson 1968

Isaacson, Walter. *Elon Musk*. New York: Simon & Schuster 2023

Weber, Max. Gesammelte Aufsätze zur Religionssoziologie, 3 Bde, Tübingen: Mohr. *Max Weber on the Methodology of the Social Sciences*, tr. and ed. Edward A. Shils and Henry A. Finch. Glencoe/Ill.: Free Press 1949

CHAPTER 12

Aesthetics, or Hegel

Abstract Like moral philosophy, aesthetic philosophy seems to investigate its objects regardless of the meaning and the reality question, falsifying, it seems, my hypothesis on philosophy. I argue that we can relate aesthetics to the meaning question, though we thus must consider *anything* a possible object of aesthetics and arts, and that we should do so, as only thus can we understand that the questions of aesthetics are fundamental and can concern everything.

This consequence fits well in with the fact that in current art anything can be an artwork, as Duchamp's ready-mades show. But if questions of aesthetics concern everything, as I presuppose, then we must assume that we can respond in a normative way to everything not only by following moral and metaphysical norms, but also by emotions, sentiments, and reflections not yet checked by morality, metaphysics, science, or another system of ideas, and that we do so in art. This assumption can be confirmed by Hegel's aesthetics.

I conclude with remarks to underline the advantage of seeing philosophy as asking two basic questions. This approach makes use of the difference between doing things heterotelically, as a means to do something else, and doing them for their own sake. If we recognize the importance, we'll understand what belongs to an acceptable answer to the meaning question.

U. Steinvorth, *A Brief Presentation of Philosophy and Its History*, https://doi.org/10.1007/978-3-031-72533-3_12

Keywords Philosophy • Aesthetics • The meaning question • Ready-
mades • Pre-normative responses • The two basic questions of
philosophy

There is still a grave objection to the hypothesis I have built this book on,
that philosophical problems explicitly or implicitly ask the reality and the
meaning question. Philosophy is divided into three parts, *theoretical philosophy* discussing problems of knowledge that can be easily understood as
reality questions, *practical philosophy* discussing problems of what we
ought to do, which with difficulty can be understood as meaning questions, and *aesthetic philosophy*, which doesn't seem understandable as
answering the meaning or reality question. For it discusses aesthetic phenomena, such as how and when nature and works of art are beautiful or
sublime or whether judgments on beauty are universally valid, regardless
of the meaning or reality question. True, we *can* ask whether what is called
aesthetic isn't an illusion, or what aesthetic phenomena mean, but this
isn't what aesthetics discusses.

My hypothesis is that to be philosophical, a question must be *fundamental*, asking how *anything* can be real or what *anything* or "it all"
means. For the same hypothesis, Leibniz (1885: 602; 1890: *Principles of
Grace*, art.7) saw in the question *Why is there* anything *rather than nothing?* the fundamental question of philosophy, and Heidegger (1953: 1;
1959· 7f) and Wittgenstein (T 6.44) repeated him. Hence, just as I interpreted moral problems as philosophical, or concerning anything, by
understanding morality as a restriction of religious and metaphysical
norms that I argued are responses to the meaning question, we should
interpret aesthetic problems as concerning anything by understanding the
objects of aesthetics, the works of art, as responses to the meaning
question.

But how then does aesthetics differ from practical philosophy? Consider
how children can ask for the meaning of "it all". Here is an example:

*Why do I have brown eyes rather than blue ones like my brother?—Because your
father has brown eyes too.—And why does my father have brown eyes?—Because
some people are born with brown and some with blue eyes.—But why?—O go to
a physicist or priest; they'll tell you why!*

The dialogue seems to start with a question for a cause, but as we see the why-questions can be repeated without end, just as we can go on asking which number comes after the greatest number we can count, we understand it as asking for the *meaning* of the fact for whose *causes* we seemed to ask. But what are we to understand by the meaning of facts? When tracing back practical philosophy to the meaning question, I supposed practical philosophy is something that can be explained as requiring us to *do* something. Yet we respond not only by *doing* something. Our first response is wonder or horror, laughing or crying, wowing or cursing. Hegel relied on this fact when he explicated, in his *Encyclopedia*, his philosophy of mind. He classified art, religion of "revelation" that is Christianity, and science that includes philosophy as forms of presenting the absolute, or God or "the idea". The absolute, which he also called *meaning* (in his *Aesthetics*, e.g. Suhrk. vol. 13: 36, 229), is immanent in history and articulated successively in art, Christianity, and science. Hegel considered only science, more exactly his own philosophy, today's adequate way to present the absolute, but art remained special.

For art was for him the first form to present the absolute. It includes the rituals of pre-Christian religion, such as mystery cults, processions, theater performances, and the building and adorning of temples. It lacks the means of presentation gained by the Christian idea of revelation (allowing the mind that philosophy both exemplifies and explores to identify with the absolute) and by concepts that enable us to do science and philosophy. It's not "the supreme mode of our knowledge of the Absolute", it "no longer fills our highest need"; we "have got beyond venerating works of art as divine". "Thought and reflection have spread their wings above fine art"; "the complicated state of civil and political life … does not permit a heart entangled in petty interests to free itself to the higher ends of art" (1975: 9f; Suhrk. vol. 13: 23f). But we may add, without adulterating Hegel's claim, that art is the *stage of truth* most adequate to a time that lacks recognized criteria of truth. Today, we doubt that anything else can be understood but facts. Whether there is anything we may call the meaning of the world, even if the meaning is understood immanently, has become dubious; hence, so has become philosophy and its meaning question.

Only art is accorded a fool's license to act as if one could seriously ponder on questions of the meaning of the world. Art has become the last stronghold of former philosophy's hope that the meaning question can be answered without presupposing a practical metaphysics or an ideology, and philosophical aesthetics can gain center stage.

I refer to Hegel to support my claim that like practical philosophy, philosophical aesthetics answers the meaning question, though not by norms that tell us *what to do* to find meaning in the world, but by pointing out how to *feel, take,* or *approach* the world to find meaning in it. I imply that the objects of aesthetics, artworks, must be understood as belonging to a way to point out how to feel and take the world to find meaning in it.

This claim can be confirmed by a fact that was a problem to all aesthetic theories, the fact that ready-mades such as Duchamp's urinal or Warhol's Brillo boxes are considered artworks, though they are identical with ordinary urinals and Brillo boxes (though Warhol specced his boxes). As Karlheinz Lüdeking (1988) has argued, ready-mades become artworks only by being *used* as artworks. All efforts to conceive art as something differing from non-art by its constitution: by its looks, essence, or the linguistic rules to identify it, founder on the famous urinal. Yet this urinal became art not by accident. Rather, as Lüdeking says, it, that is, its use, needs "qualities like that of being witty or ingenious" (179, cp. 176); it must "seem to us meaningful" (203). As a use can be meaningful only if we relate it to something of which it reveals meaning, the urinal could become art only because the public or art critics related its use to what it seemed to them to indicate about the meaning of the society in which it was used.

It wasn't just the urinal that became art but its use as an exhibition object that questions the exhibition business, suggesting that there is more in art and the meaning it may express than can be expressed in the exhibition business. Yet understanding art as a way to use *anything* distinctly from the way things are used in Christianity and in science, philosophical aesthetics becomes fundamental, as it is understood as relating to anything. Hence, insisting that philosophy answers the meaning or the reality question secures to philosophy the quality of explaining "it all".

I conclude with three remarks. *First,* as we are ordinarily engaged in practical work, we often forget what aesthetics can tell us: that non-practical aesthetic responses to the facts we face are a most elementary part of our life. One way to remember this part is to bear in mind that today, we often do things for something else but that if we don't do anything autotelically, our life is in vain, as Aristotle stated (NE I 1094a21). Or as Russell mocked:

The modern man thinks that everything ought to be done for the sake of something else, and never for its own sake. Serious-minded persons, for example, are continually condemning the habit of going to the cinema, and telling us that it leads the young into crime. But all the work that goes to producing a cinema is respectable, because it is work, and because it brings a money profit. (1935/2005: 11)

Note that Russell implies what also Weber implies, that aesthetic responses have the special property of being autotelic. Schopenhauer, quoted approvingly by Danto (1997: 81), pointed to this property explicitly:

...the work of genius may be music, philosophy, painting, or poetry; it is nothing for use or profit. To be useless and unprofitable is one of the characteristics of works of genius; it is their patent of nobility. All other human works exist only for the maintenance and relief of our existence; only those here discussed do not; they alone exist for their own sake, and are to be regarded in this sense as the flower ... of existence. (1958, 2: 388)

The flower of existence are activities done for their own sake *and* worth doing so. The rest exists for them. But Russell and Schopenhauer don't clarify when an action is not only done for its own sake but also worth doing so. This missing point is clarified by Weber's understanding of value spheres, which leads me to my *second remark*.

Value sphere activities are done for their own sake, but unlike twiddling one's thumbs that we can also do autotelically they are considered worth doing. They are thus considered if, I assumed, they are done in a value sphere. For this, there are at least two conditions: the activities are (1) done in a community of agents who share the passion for the sphere-specific goal and cooperate and compete in coming as close to the goal as possible and are (2) measured by a standard of perfection that the agents discover in their activities (cp. Steinvorth 2023, Ch. 19–22). These standards are often difficult to define but indicate a perfection that makes actions pursuing them worth doing. They also exclude that the worth of the action is subjective or invented rather than objective and discovered.

Thus, as Weber might insist, in science perfection is *found* in theories enabling us to make unexpected predictions, in the economy in exchanges saving resources, in politics in efficient ways of managing public affairs. The perfection standards of art and eroticism are controversial, but most artists laugh at the idea that their standard is determined by convention or by necessities of nature or society, rather than by what they discover to be true art, and Don Giovanni would laugh no less at the idea that his erotic perfection standard is not what he discovers in his adventures. Scientists and the agents of the sphere of justice enforcement, judges and lawyers, can also insist on the sphere-born objective validity of their standards of truth and rightness.

The *third remark* is that the activities of any value sphere unite properties of actions that many people consider most attractive. There hasn't been much debate on what *actions* people love most. Theorists have rather thought about *states* that satisfy us most, such as happiness, fame, or power. But there is consonance about some qualities of attractive actions. They must (1) be done for their own sake, as heterotelic actions leave us without meaning; (2) be cooperative, as we want to connect to other people with the same passions regardless of their race, religion, or gender; but (3) leave us a place for competing with other people who see the same goal as worth pursuing. For we don't want just somehow to contribute to some perfection but to distinguish ourselves by the special achievements we prove capable of. Competitiveness is considered bourgeois, as bourgeois praise it as stimulated by and stimulating market exchange. Yet some degree of it is loved in most societies, so it can't be only a bourgeois preference. Finally, actions must (4) allow us to cooperate and compete also with the dead who have shared, and with future minds who will share our interest in one of the many values there are.

If we prefer such attractive actions to aiming at the grand ideas of ideologists and philosophers such as liberty or happiness, this doesn't mean that we needn't care for the future. On the contrary, we'll have to look for a politics that allows everyone to choose their value sphere. This requires replacing states with a global administration, and traditional liberalism and democracy with institutions more apt to check power. Thus, this very short presentation of philosophy includes mapping a way into a future that can answer the two questions of philosophy and presents a kind of activity that exploits its potential rather than neutering it.

LITERATURE

Danto, Arthur. *After the End of Art. Contemporary Art and the Pale of History*, Princeton: Princeton UP 1997

Heidegger, Martin. *Einführung in die Metaphysik*. Tübingen: Niemeyer 1953

Heidegger, Martin. Einführung in die Metaphysik. Tübingen: Niemeyer. *Introduction to Metaphysics*. New Haven: Yale UP 1959

Hegel, G.W.F. Philosophy of Spirit (part 3 of his Encyclopaedia of the Philosophical Sciences. *Aesthetics. Lectures on Fine Arts*. Tr. E.M. Knox. Vol. 1. New York: Oxford UP 1975

Leibniz, Gottfried Wilhelm. The Monadology. *Die philosophischen Schriften von Gottfried Wilhelm Leibniz VI.* Ed. C.J. Gerhardt, Berlin: Weidmannsche Buchh. 1885

Leibniz, Gottfried Wilhelm. The Monadology. *The philosophical works of Leibnitz: comprising the Monadology … Principles of nature and of grace*, ed. G.M. Duncan, New Haven: Tuttle 1890

Lüdeking, Karlheinz. *Analytische Philosophie der Kunst*. Frankfurt: Athenäum 1988

Russell, Bertrand. *In Praise of Idleness and Other Essays* (1935). London: Routledge 2005

Schopenhauer, Arthur. *The World as Will and Representation*, tr. E.F.G. Payne, New York: Hafner 1958

Steinvorth, Ulrich. "Zur Legitimität des Klonens." In Ludger Schwarte, Hg., Körper und Recht: anthropologische Dimensionen der Rechtsphilosophie. München: Fink. *Unterdrückung durch Beglückung. Eine liberale Revision der politischen Philosophie*. Hamburg: Meiner 2023

LITERATURE

Adams, Douglas. *The Hitchhiker's Guide to the Galaxy: The Original Radio Scripts.* London: Pan Books 1985

Albritton, Rogers. "Freedom of Will and Freedom of Action". *Proceedings and Addresses of the American Philosophical Association*, 59, 1985, pp. 239–251

Aristotle. *The Complete Works.* Ed. Jonathan Barnes. Princeton, NJ: Princeton UP 1984

Aron, Raymond. *Democracy and totalitarianism* (French orig. 1965). London: Weidenfeld and Nicolson 1968

Augustine. *Civitas Dei.* Tr. Marcus Dods. Augustine of Hippo St - City of God. pdf Obtained Oct. 11, 2023

———. A Treatise of Grace and Will. In *From Nicene and Post-Nicene Fathers*, ser. 1, ed. P. Schaff, vol. 5. Buffalo: Christian Literature Publishing 1887

Austin, John L. *How to Do Things With Words.* Cambridge/Mass. 1962

Bobzien, Susanne. *Determinism, Freedom, and Moral Responsibility. Essays in Ancient Philosophy.* Oxford: OUP 2021

Bostrom, Nick. "Are you living in a computer simulation?" *Philosophical Quarterly* 53, 2003, 243–55

Bühler, Karl. *Die geistige Entwicklung des Kindes.* Jena: Fischer 1918

———. *Sprachtheorie. Die Darstellungsfunktion der Sprache.* Jena: Fischer 1934

Byrne, Christopher. *Aristotle's Science of Matter and Motion.* Toronto: University of Toronto Pr. 2018

Calderon de la Barca, Pedro. *La vida es sueño (Life is a dream)* Madrid 1636

Camus, Albert. *L'homme révolté.* Paris: Gallimard 1951

© The Author(s), under exclusive license to Springer Nature Switzerland AG 2024

U. Steinvorth, *A Brief Presentation of Philosophy and Its History*, https://doi.org/10.1007/978-3-031-72533-3

88   LITERATURE

Chadwick, Henry. *Augustine: A Very Short Introduction.* New York: Oxford UP 1986/2001.
Chomsky, Noam. "A Review of B. F. Skinner's Verbal Behavior". *Language* 35, 1959, pp. 26–58.
Danto, Arthur. *After the End of Art. Contemporary Art and the Pale of History,* Princeton: Princeton UP 1997
Dawkins, Richard. *Science in the Soul: Selected Writing of a Passionate Rationalist.* London: Bantam 2017
Descartes, René. *Meditations on First Philosophy: With Selections from the Objections and Replies,* Cambridge: Cambridge UP, tr. Cottingham, 1996
Destutt de Tracy, Antoine Louis Claude. *A Treatise on Political Economy or Elements of Ideology,* ed. by Thomas Jefferson 1817, reprint New York: Kelley 1970
Durkheim, Emile. *De la division du travail social.* Paris: Alcan, 1893
Ekenberg, Tomas. "Free Will and Free Action in Anselm of Canterbury". *History of Philosophy Quarterly* 22, 2005, pp. 301–318
Emilsson, Eyjólfur Kjalar. "Leibniz, Plato, Plotinus." In Karfík, Filip and Euree Song, eds., *Plato Revived.* Berlin: de Gruyter, 2013
Epictetus, *Discourses. Tr. George Long.* New York: Appleton 1904
Feynman, Richard. *The Meaning of it All. Thoughts of a Citizen-Scientist,* Boston: Addison-Wesley 1998 (including lectures held in 1963)
Frede, Michael. *Essays in Ancient Philosophy,* University of Minnesota Press, Minneapolis, 1987
———. *A Free Will: Origins of the Notion in Ancient Thought.* Ed. A. A. Long. Oakland: Univ. of California Pr. 2011
Frege, Gottlob. "Sinn und Bedeutung" (1892). In *Funktion, Begriff, Bedeutung.* Ed. G. Patzig, Göttingen: Vandenhoeck 1962, 38–63
———. "Der Gedanke" (1919). In *Logische Untersuchungen.* Ed. G. Patzig. Göttingen: Vandenhoeck 1966, 30–53
Görler, Woldemar. "Asthenês synkatathesis: Zur stoischen Erkenntnistheorie". *Würzburger Jahrbücher für die Altertumswissenschaft,* N.F. 3; 1977, 83–92. Reprint in *Kleine Schriften zur hellenistisch-römischen Philosophie;* ed. C. Catrein, Philosophia antiqua 95, Leiden/Boston 2004: 1–15
Habermas, Jürgen. "Genetische Sklavenherrschaft? Moralische Grenzen reproduktionsmedizinischer Fortschritte". *Die postnationale Konstellation.* Frankfurt: Suhrkamp, 1998, pp. 243–247
Haynes, J-D. "Beyond Libet", in A. Clark, J. Kiverstein, T. Vierkant, Hg., *Decomposing the Will,* Oxford: Oxford University Press 2013
Head, Brian. *Ideology and Social Science: Destutt de Tracy and French Liberalism.* Dordrecht: M. Nijhoff 1985
Heidegger, Martin. *Einführung in die Metaphysik.* Tübingen: Niemeyer 1953
———. *Introduction to Metaphysics.* New Haven: Yale UP 1959

Hegel, G.W.F. *Philosophy of Spirit* (part 3 of his *Encyclopaedia of the Philosophical Sciences,* 1830), https://antilogicalism.com/wp-content/uploads/2016/12/hegel_mind_final.pdf, 2016. Obtained Oct. 11, 2023

———. *Aesthetics. Lectures on Fine Arts.* Tr. E.M. Knox. Vol. 1. New York: Oxford UP 1975

———. n.d. *Werke in zwanzig Bänden.* Frankfurt: Suhrkamp 1969ff, abbr. *Suhrk*

Hitler, Adolf. Mein Kampf. 2 Bde. München: Franz Eher 1925 and 1927. Quoted from the ed. of 1943

Hobbes, Thomas. *Leviathan* (1651), ed. Macpherson, Penguin 1968, abbr. *Lev*

Hume, David. *A Treatise of Human Nature,* ed. Selby-Bigge and Nidditch, Oxford: Clarendon Press (1740) 1978

———. *Dialogues Concerning Natural Religion* (1748). New York: Hafner 1948

Huxley, Aldous. *Brave new World,* London: Chatto and Windus 1932

Huxley, Thomas Henry. "On the hypothesis that animals are automata, and its history". *Fortnightly Review* 22, 1874, pp. 555–580. Reprint in *Method and Results*: Essays by Thomas H. Huxley, New York: Appleton, 1898

Iggers, Georg. "The Idea of Progress: A Critical Reassessment", *The American Historical Review* 71, 1965, pp. 1–17

Isaacson, Walter. *Elon Musk.* New York: Simon & Schuster 2023

Jonas, Hans. "Gnosis and Modern Nihilism", *Social Research* 19, 1952, 430–52

———. *Das Prinzip Verantwortung—Versuch einer Ethik für die technologische Zivilisation.* Frankfurt: Suhrkamp 1979

Kant, Immanuel. n.d. *Gesammelte Werke.* Berlin: Königlich Preußische Akademie der Wissenschaften, Berlin 1900ff

———. *Critique of Pure Reason* (1781, 2nd ed. 1787), tr. Paul Guyer and A.W. Wood, Cambridge: Cambridge UP, 1998, abbr. A for the first edition, B for the second edition; their pagination is given also in Guyer and Wood's edition

———. *Groundwork for the Metaphysics of Morals,* ed. and tr. Allen W. Wood, Yale UP, Wood 2002a

———. *Critique of Practical Reason* (1789). Tr. Pluhar. Indianapolis/Cambridge: Hackett 2002b

———. *The Metaphysics of Morals,* tr. Mary Gregor. New York: Cambridge UP 1991

Kafka, Franz. "Die Verwandlung". *Die weißen Blätter,* ed. René Schickele. Oct. 1915

Kipling, Rudyard. "The White Man's Burden". *London Times,* 4.2.1899, *New York Tribune* und *The Sun* 5.2. 1899

Kirk, G.S., and J.E. Raven, *The Presocratic Philosophers. A Critical History with a Selection of Texts.* Cambridge: Cambridge UP 1966 (abbr. K&R)

Koyré, Alexandre. *From the Closed World to the Infinite Universe,* Baltimore: John Hopkins Pr. 1957

Lehmann, Max. *Preußen und die katholische Kirche seit 1640.* 2. Theil 1740–1747. Leipzig: Hirzel, 1881

Leibniz, Gottfried Wilhelm. *The Monadology* (1714). Tr. Nicholas Rescher. University of Pittsburgh Pr 1991

———. *Die philosophischen Schriften von Gottfried Wilhelm Leibniz VI.* Ed. C.J. Gerhardt, Berlin: Weidmannsche Buchh. 1885

———. *The philosophical works of Leibnitz: comprising the Monadology ... Principles of nature and of grace*, ed. G.M. Duncan, New Haven: Tuttle 1890

Libet, Benjamin. "Unconscious cerebral initiative and the role of conscious will in voluntary action". *The Behavioral and Brain Sciences* 8, 1985, 529–566

Libet, Benjamin; Wright, E. W.; Feinstein, B.; Pearl, D. K. "Subjective Referral of the Timing for a Conscious Sensory Experience". *Brain* 102, 1979, 191–22

Lichtenberg, Georg Christoph. *Schriften und Briefe.* Bd. 2. München: Hanser 1991

Locke, John. *Two Treatises of Government*, ed. Laslett, Cambridge: Cambridge UP 1960. Abbr. *Tr.* The numbers of the paragraphs refer to the Second Treatise

Lovejoy, Arthur Oncken. *The Great Chain of Being: A Study of the History of an Idea*, Cambridge: Harvard UP 1936

Lüdeking, Karlheinz. *Analytische Philosophie der Kunst.* Frankfurt: Athenäum 1988

McKenna, Michael, "Compatibilism", *Stanford Encyclopedia of Philosophy* 2019

Marx, Karl, and Friedrich Engels. *The Communist Manifesto.* 1848/2010. https://www.marxists.org/archive/marx/works/download/pdf/Manifesto.pdf. Obtained Oct. 11, 2023

Mauthner, Fritz. *Beiträge zu einer Kritik der Sprache* (1913), Leipzig: Librorium Editions 2019, Bd. 3

Mayr, Ernst. *The Growth of Biological Thought. Diversity, Evolution, and Inheritance.* Cambridge/MA: Harvard UP 1982

———. *One Long Argument. Charles Darwin and the Genesis of Modern Evolutionary Thought.* Cambridge/MA: Harvard UP 1991

Moore, G.E. *Principia Ethica.* Cambridge: Cambridge UP (1903), 1962

Moravcszik, John. "Aristotle's Theory of Categories", in J.M. ed., *Aristotle. A Collection of Critical Essays,* New York 1967, 125–45

Musk, Elon. https://www.youtube.com/watch?v=xBKRuI2zHp0- Obtained Oct. 11, 2023

Nagel, Thomas. "What is it like to be a bat?" In *Mortal Questions.* New York: Cambridge UP 1979, 165–180

———. *What Does it All Mean? A Very Short Introduction to Philosophy.* New York: Oxford UP 1987

Nietzsche, Friedrich. *Sämtliche Werke.* Kritische Studienausgabe. München: dtv 1980

Nozick, Robert. *Philosophical Explanations.* Clarendon Press, Oxford 1981

Pals, Daniel. *Nine Theories of Religion,* New York: Oxford UP 2015

Pargament, Kenneth. *The Psychology of Religion and Coping. Theory, Research, Practice.* New York: Guilford Pr. 1997

Pascal, Blaise. *Pensées and Other Writings,* ed. Levi. Oxford: Oxford UP 1995

Pellegrin, Pierre. *Animals in the World. Five Essays on Aristotle's Biology*, Albany: SUNY Pr. 2023

Plato, *Complete Works*, ed. John M. Cooper and D.S. Hutchinson. Indianapolis: Hackett, 1997

Plotinus. *Enneads* in seven volumes. Cambridge/Mass. Harvard UP 1988

Popper, Karl. *Objective Knowledge*. Oxford: Clarendon 1972,

Putnam, Hilary. *Reason, Truth, and History*. New York: Cambridge UP 1981

Russell, Bertrand. *In Praise of Idleness and Other Essays* (1935). London: Routledge 2005

Schopenhauer, Arthur. *The World as Will and Representation*, tr. E.F.G. Payne, New York: Hafner 1958

———. *Preisschrift über die Grundlage der Moral* (1841), in *Werke in zehn Bänden*, Band VI, Zürich 1977

Schultze-Kraft, M., ... Haynes, J.-D. "The point of no return in vetoing self-initiated movements". *Proceedings of the National Academy of Sciences*, 113(4), 2015, 1080–1085

Skinner, B.F. *Verbal Behavior*. New York: Appleton-Century-Crofts 1957

Smart, J.J.C., and Haldane, John. *Atheism and Theism*, Oxford: Blackwell 2003

Spangler, O. A. "Aristotle's Criticism of Parmenides in Physics I". *Apeiron*, 13(2), 1979, 92–103, 92

Steinvorth, Ulrich. "Zur Legitimität des Klonens." In Ludger Schwarte, Hg., *Körper und Recht: anthropologische Dimensionen der Rechtsphilosophie*. München: Fink 2003, 289–302

———. *The Metaphysics of Modernity*, Milwaukee: Marquette UP 2013

———. *A Secular Absolute. How Modern Philosophy Discovered Authenticity*. Palgrave Macmillan, New York 2020

———. *Unterdrückung durch Beglückung. Eine liberale Revision der politischen Philosophie*. Hamburg: Meiner 2023

Summerell, O. F. "Self-Causality from Plotinus to Eckhart and from Descartes to Kant". *Quaestio 2*, 2002, 493–518

Terrell, Timothy D. *Introduction* to Destutt de Tracy 1817

Torpey, John. "Max Weber and the Idea of Progress". *Max Weber Studies* 19, 2019, pp. 88–105

de Waal, Frans. https://www.youtube.com/watch?v=meiU6TxysCg (2013). Obtained July 30, 2023

Weber, Max. *Gesammelte Aufsätze zur Religionssoziologie*, 3 Bde, Tübingen: Mohr 1920–1921 (in vol. 1 *Vorbemerkung* pp. 1–16 and *Zwischenbetrachtung*, abbr. *Zw*, pp. 536–73)

———. Prefatory Remarks. Tr. Stephen Kalberg. In Stephen Kalberg, *The Protestant Ethic and the Spirit of Capitalism*. New York: Routledge 2001a, 149–64

————. The Protestant Ethic and the Spirit of Capitalism. (1905). Translated by Parsons in 1930. Reedited by Routledge, London 2001; https://selforganizedseminar.wordpress.com/wpcontent/uploads/2011/07/weber_protestant_ethic.pdf

————. *Economic Ethics of World Religions* (1920), ed. G. Roth and C. Wittich: University of California Pr 1978

————. *Wirtschaft und Gesellschaft* (1922). Tübingen: Mohr 1980 (abbr. WG)

————. *The Protestant Ethic and the Spirit of Capitalism*, tr. T. Parsons, German orig. 1905, New York: Routledge 2001b

————. *Economy and Society*, ed. and tr. Keith Tribe, Cambridge/MA: Harvard UP 2019 (abbr. ES)

————. *Max Weber on the Methodology of the Social Sciences*, tr. and ed. Edward A. Shils and Henry A. Finch. Glencoe/Ill.: Free Press 1949

————. *From Max Weber: Essays in Sociology*. Ed. H.H. Gerth and C. Wright Mills. New York: Oxford UP 1946

Wittgenstein, Ludwig. *Tractatus logico-philosophicus*. In Schriften. Frankfurt/M: Suhrkamp 1960 (abbr. T)

————. *Philosophical Investigations*, Oxford: Blackwell 1963 (abbrev. PI)

————. *Wittgenstein's Lectures, Cambridge 1932–1933*, ed. A. Ambrose. Oxford: Blackwell 1979

Wladika, Michael. "Aspects of Hegel's Interpretation of Plotinus". *Hegel-Jahrbuch* 2015, 124–131

INDEX

U. Steinvorth, *A Brief Presentation of Philosophy and Its History*,
https://doi.org/10.1007/978-3-031-72533-3

GPSR Compliance

The European Union's (EU) General Product Safety Regulation (GPSR) is a set of rules that requires consumer products to be safe and our obligations to ensure this.

If you have any concerns about our products, you can contact us on ProductSafety@springernature.com

In case Publisher is established outside the EU, the EU authorized representative is:

Springer Nature Customer Service Center GmbH
Europaplatz 3
69115 Heidelberg, Germany

The manufacturer's authorised representative in the EU is Springer
Nature Customer Service Centre GmbH, Europaplatz 3, 69115 Heidelberg,
Germany. If you have any concerns regarding our products, please
contact ProductSafety@springernature.com

Printed and bound by CPI Group (UK) Ltd, Croydon, CR0 4YY
29/04/2026
02099538-0003